# Drama and CLIL

D1717437

# Linguistic Insights

Studies in Language and Communication

Edited by Maurizio Gotti,
University of Bergamo

Volume 194

PETER LANG
Bern · Berlin · Bruxelles · Frankfurt am Main · New York · Oxford · Wien

Susana Nicolás Román & Juan José Torres Núñez (eds)

# Drama and CLIL

· · · · · · · · · · · · · · · · · · · ·

## A new challenge for the teaching approaches in bilingual education

PETER LANG

Bern · Berlin · Bruxelles · Frankfurt am Main · New York · Oxford · Wien

**Bibliographic information published by die Deutsche Nationalbibliothek**
Die Deutsche Nationalbibliothek lists this publication in the Deutsche National-
bibliografie; detailed bibliographic data is available on the Internet
at ‹http://dnb.d-nb.de›.

British Library Cataloguing-in-Publication Data: A catalogue record for this book
is available from The British Library, Great Britain

Library of Congress Control Number: 2015936242

ISSN 1424-8689 pb.                    ISSN 2235-6371 eBook
ISBN 978-3-0343-1629-3 pb.           ISBN 978-3-0351-0832-3 eBook

This publication has been peer reviewed.

© Peter Lang AG, International Academic Publishers, Bern 2015
Hochfeldstrasse 32, CH-3012 Bern, Switzerland
info@peterlang.com, www.peterlang.com

Printed in Switzerland

*Drama is a tool of reality which makes reality
a tool of humanness*

Edward Bond, Notebook, 6/ 2/11

# Contents

LENI DAM

# Foreword

## Drama and CLIL – and Language Learner Autonomy: A personal experience

When I was asked to write an introduction to this book, I immediately accepted. Even though I am not a specialist, neither in CLIL, nor as a teacher of drama, I am a strong believer in making use of these two educational approaches when it comes to good language learning. The chapters included here definitely support this belief. They provide the reader with excellent examples of different ways of working with drama and CLIL. They show that among many other positive effects "the two approaches motivate students through engagement and connection, but they are also connected in their holistic nature, engaging the whole learner in the learning process" (Hillyard, in this volume). When looking at the examples, though, I find it striking that a third approach – namely language learner autonomy (LLA) – where learners are expected to "be in charge of their own learning" (Holec 1981: 3) is almost lacking. In most cases, the examples given and activities suggested are teacher-directed and lend themselves to a large extent to rather traditional *language teaching and learning methods*. As neither drama nor CLIL are committed to any methodological language learning approach, Dieter Wolff (Wolff 2011: 71) points to this possible tendency: "teachers often tend to fall back on rather traditional language learning methods arguing, for example, that content subjects cannot be learned without a terminology which needs to be acquired through learning lists of words". A possible solution could be to embed CLIL as well as

Drama in a learner-centered concept of effective language learning and teaching – autonomous language learning.[1]

In order to support this view, I will start out by defining learner autonomy as well as describe the cornerstones in the development of language learner autonomy. I shall then go on to mention points of contact between these cornerstones and the examples of drama and CLIL in the book – in order to make the suggestion of embedment feasible. The example of *Making a play* in an autonomy class consisting of beginners in a Danish comprehensive school hopefully underpins the suggestion. I will finish with a few concluding remarks.

## Defining language learner autonomy

The term *learner autonomy* was first coined in 1979 by Henri Holec (Holec 1981: 3). Many definitions have since been given to the term, depending on the writer and the context. For this introduction I have chosen to use the so-called *Bergen definition,* which adds the social aspect of (language) learning to Holec's definition:

> Learner autonomy is characterized by a readiness to take charge of one's own learning in the service of one's needs and purposes. This entails a capacity and willingness to act independently and in co-operation with others, as a socially responsible person. An autonomous learner is an active participant in the social processes of learning, but also an active interpreter of new information in terms of what she/he already and uniquely knows (qtd. in Dam 1995: 1–2)[2]

The concept *language learner autonomy* stresses the view that the learner's agency is – as far as possible – channelled through the target language in the autonomous language learning environment (cf. O'Rourke / Carson 2010).

---

1    The LAALE project (*Language Acquisition in an Autonomous Learning Environment*) provides evidence of the effectiveness of autonomous language learning. See for example Legenhausen 2003, 2009.

2    The *Bergen-definition* saw the light during a Nordic Workshop held in Bergen in 1990.

## Developing language learner autonomy

In the process of making learners willing to take charge of their own learning and capable of doing so (cf. the *Bergen-definition* above), it has turned out that the following key-issues – or cornerstones – in the organisation of the autonomy classroom are of utmost importance.[3]

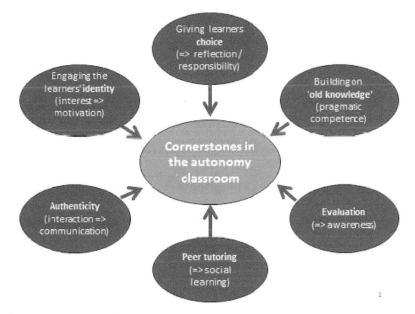

Figure 1. Cornerstones in the autonomy classroom.

---

3    For more literature on developing learner autonomy, see for example Little (1991), Dam (1995), Benson (2001).

## Points of contact between Autonomous Language Learning (ALL) and Drama and CLIL

Even though the examples of drama and CLIL in this book do not incorporate learner autonomy as a general concept, most of the cornerstones in the autonomy classroom:

1. engaging the learners' identity and thus their interest and motivation,
2. authenticity when it comes to interaction and communication,
3. building on "old knowledge" and thus activating their pragmatic competence,
4. giving learners choice in order to make them reflect and in this way responsible for the choices made, and
5. social learning,

are well represented. The few quotes below are intended to illustrate the points of contact between the three approaches. They are taken from the chapter by Susan Hillyard, *The Question of Connection: Connecting Drama and CLIL as Motivating Forces in the Classroom* and the chapter by Nailya Garipova, *Linking theatre to CLIL in Secondary schools: Bilingual Context Plays*, but they could easily be extracted from other chapters.

In her introduction Susan Hillyard points at the importance of bridging real life with the classroom and thus give the learners a chance to make use of *old knowledge*: "The word 'connection' in the title thus refers to the connection between the two disciplines [Drama and CLIL] and to the way in which both act as motivating forces for students in language classrooms by helping them to make the connections they need between their real lives and classroom life". When it comes to *identity and motivation* she refers to Hadfield and Dornyei (2010): "If the person we would like to become speaks an L2, the *ideal L2 self* is a powerful motivator to learn the L2".

Naylia Garipova, among others, sees working with theatre as a possibility "to create the working atmosphere needed to stimulate the pupils' *motivation and cooperation*". When working with the type of theatre in question, *bilingual plays,* she adheres to a number of principles – 12 in all – from which I will mention two dealing with *choice*: "All the students of the group can take part in the adaptation and elaboration of the plays. They will choose the parts voluntarily". And: "The theme of the play should be interesting and amusing and must be chosen by the pupils" (Garipova, in this volume).

Under the heading 'Classroom implementations', Garipova writes: "After having adapted and staged different plays, my students of the fourth year of Compulsory Secondary Education talked to me and showed the desire to create their own play". From here on, she describes her students' creation of their own play – where the cornerstones of the autonomy classroom, apart from integrated evaluation, are at play. Therefore, why not start from the very beginning of learning English? This is an example of the difference between a teacher-directed teaching environment and a learner-directed and -centred learning-environment. In the autonomy classroom the learners do not have to 'learn' to make a play. Quite the opposite. In order to engage and activate the learners from the very first day of learning English, the knowledge that they bring to the classroom is made use of – in this connection their knowledge about stories, plays and plots in everyday life as in the example below.

## An example of autonomous language learning at beginners' level

Getting learners actively involved in their own learning i.e. developing learner autonomy in an educational context, is in many cases a long and difficult process for learners as well as educators. It is difficult for learners who have been used to being spoon-fed in previous teaching/learning situations, but it is especially difficult for teachers who are afraid of losing control of the learning process. For both parties it is a question of accepting that 'small is beautiful' – of taking small steps of 'letting go' and 'taking hold' (Page, 1992).

In order to cope with these difficulties, the teacher in her role as the one to stimulate and support learning must gradually introduce possible activities – one at a time. These activities have, on the one hand, to be within the curricular demands for the linguistic development of her learners. On the other hand, they have to give scope for the cornerstones in the autonomy classroom (cf. above). The learners on their part will be asked to try out these activities and evaluate them according to whether they like them or not and whether they find them useful for their individual needs. At beginners' level these evaluations are initiated and guided by the teacher.

As regards the curricular demands for proficiency in expressing oneself, some of the very first activities introduced at beginners' level in my classes were:

1.   Questions and answers in pairs: student produced individual questions that the questioner did not know the answer to and which thus supports the notion of authenticity.
2.   Picture + text: find a picture and make a text individually or in pairs, giving scope for choice, L1-knowledge, cooperation.
3.   Two minutes' talk: small talk in pairs about topics chosen by the students themselves and carried out in the target language as far as possible. This allows the learners to bring in their identity apart from supporting social learning and genuine authentic communication.
4.   Make a play: self-created plot, story-line, and dialogue. In the class in question (see below) this activity was initiated by one of the learners. As can be seen, all the cornerstones are involved.
5.   Make a game: learner-produced games to be played among the learners themselves, such as dominoes, picture lotto, board-games.

The activities were entered on a poster and extended with new ideas either from the teacher or from the students themselves (cf. number 4 above) to choose from. These *simple* activities – simple in the sense that the instructions were very easy to follow – continued to be used all through the five years at secondary school as they had the characteristics of a *good* activity i.e. everyone could add to the activity and everyone would gain from taking part in that (differentiation). Furthermore, all the cornerstones are at play. In addition, the outcome – or the products – of these activities were not at all simple, on the contrary, they were quite complex. Over the years, the content and the format would change: *Picture + text* would develop into newspaper articles, brochures, reports. The *two minutes' talk* would develop into long discussions; *make a play* would develop into various forms for drama produced by the learners themselves and *make a game* would develop into quite sophisticated types of board-games such as *Trivial Pursuit* with rules set up by the learners. Today they would probably produce computer-games.

## *An example of 'Make a play': a personal experience*

The following example of a student-produced play, *OH NO!!!!!*, is taken from the first year of English[4]. The work on the play started after approximately eight weeks of English – four lessons a week of forty-five minutes. The students, three boys and one girl, were all eleven years old at the time and of mixed ability – L. being the weakest student in class and K. the strongest. It was K. who came up with the idea and from his logbook entries it can be seen that he had worked on the idea at home, before sharing it with a group. On Wednesday, 21 October, he entered into his logbook:

---

Wednesday, 21st October

1. Sing a song
2. Share homework
3. Make a play with: Helene, Morten, Lars, Lasse
4. Homework: Make a play
5. Comments:

    det var drøngodt. Hvorfor? det ved jeg ikke. det var det bare.

    [It was fantastic. Why? I don't know. That is just how it was. – my translation]

---

Figure 2. Extract from K's logbook.

---

4    For details about the work with this class, see Dam 1995: 8–32

From that day on, the group developed the play together in class. K. voluntccrcd to bc sccrctary as he had started the play and was the best at writing at this point. When working with the play in class, new words needed for the play were entered into the logbooks. Examples of vocabulary entered were: *towards, sudden, frightened, meetings, teased*[5]. From the logbook entries of the group it can be seen that they considered new ideas for the play as homework – homework being decided by the learners themselves. After a month, on Monday, 23 November, K. writes under comments: "It has been a good lesson because we got finish with our play". It is noticeable that by now the target language is used.

It might seem a long time to produce a play. However, it has to be taken into account that producing the play was only one activity out of many during this period. During the lessons there would also be joint activities for the whole class. Sharing homework with a partner was, for example, a must; watching a video in class, sing songs, etc. would all be part of lessons.

On Monday, 30 November, the play was shown to the rest of the class as well as to another class. K. had as homework made a type-written version which was distributed to the audience after the performance.

*Comments on the product*

The group has created a social reality which mirrors the daily lives of 11- year olds: school, friendship, relationship between boys and girls, bullying, solidarity and humour. The topics emanate from what they have experienced and find interesting. The learners have brought in their identity in the constructive processes resulting in an L2 text (see Garipova).

Furthermore, when it comes to language learning, then the processes underlying the text, i.e. the interactions resulting in the text itself, are of even greater value. It is in these interactions and negotiations that the learners speak as themselves. Furthermore, while building up the

---

5    For the acquisition of vocabulary in an autonomous learning environment, see Dam/Legenhausen (1996).

text, a host of authentic speech acts are carried out: they come up with suggestions, which are either accepted or rejected, the appropriateness of vocabulary is discussed and plot structure and meanings are negotiated. Even though the negotiations and discussions at this point – after two months of learning English – take place in L1, then the result is an L2 text.

*Evaluation – the pivot of learner autonomy[6]*

Whenever something was presented in class, peer-evaluation would take place. After the performance at the end of a lesson, the peers therefore entered their evaluations of the play into their respective logbooks[7]. Here are some examples from different peers:

- *S: See a play called "oh no". It has been a ggod Play for de de var gode til det* [- because they were good at it].
- *J: Set* [seen] *a play call "oh NO" det var meget godt* [it was very good].
- *M: See a Play called "Oh No". Jeg syntes det var godt og sjovt fordi M. og L. blev mobbet* [I think that it was good and funny because M. and L were bullied].
- *N: See a play called "Oh NO!" Komator fra N.* [comment from N] *Det var meget godt. Jeg forstod det meste af det.* [It was very good. I could understand most of it].

Admittedly, the evaluations are short; they are very often in L1, but they are there! Furthermore, they show that learners are capable of setting up their own criteria for a 'good play': "I could understand it, the actors were good, it was fun, it showed real life (bullying)". In the following lessons it will be up to the teacher to see to it that these peer-evaluations are made use of in the development of self-evaluation, peer-evaluation and in the process of making a play.

---

6     See Dam 1995: 49.
7     Many of my learners left their logbooks with me when leaving school, saying: "You can use them in your teacher education if you want to".

## Concluding remarks

As described above, *Making a play* is an example of authentic language use which has for quite some time now been considered the crucible of language learning. When producing a play – also as described above – language learning is taking place in an intensity which the mere performance of a play cannot achieve.

When it comes to including CLIL in the autonomy classroom,[8] it is noticeable that the product and thus the content of the learner-directed activities derives and develops from the learners' interests and the knowledge that they bring to the learning environment at the time of learning. One group at intermediate level would for example make a small book on *Hitler's Childhood* (history). Another group would create a game of *Trivial Pursuit* with questions concerned with geography, biology, history, etc. In short, the autonomous learners are active agents of their own learning, not only when it comes to language.

It is my hope that this introduction will incite teachers, teacher-trainers, and researchers of Drama and CLIL to implement elements and principles of learner autonomy (LA) and/or language learner autonomy (LLA) in their educational environments in order to combine the blessings of the three approaches.

## References

Benson, Ph. 2011 [2001]. *Teaching and Researching Autonomy in Language Learning.* 2nd ed. Harlow: Longman/Pearson.

Dam, L. 2014 [1995]. *Learner Autonomy 3. From Theory to Classroom Practice.* Dublin: Authentik/ Karlslunde: Askeladden,

Dam, L. / Legenhausen, L. 1996. The acquisition of vocabulary in an autonomous language learning environment – the first months of beginning English. In R. Pemberton et al, (ed). *Taking*

---

8        For further arguments, see e.g. Wolff (2003, 2011).

*Control – Autonomy in Language Learning*. Hong Kong: Hong Kong University Press, 265–280.

Holec, H. 1981 [1979]. *Autonomy and Foreign Language Learning.* Oxford: Pergamon.

Legenhausen, L. 2003. Second language acquisition in an autonomous learning environment. In D. Little/ J.Ridley/ E. Ushioda (eds). *Learner Autonomy in the Foreign Language Classroom – Teacher, Learner, Curriculum and Assessment.* Dublin: Trinity College Dublin, 65–77.

Legenhausen, L. 2009. Autonomous language learning. In K. Knapp/ B. Seidlhofereds. (eds). *Handbook of Applied Linguistics. Vol. 6: Foreign Language Communication and Learning.* Berlin: Mouton de Gruyter, 373 – 400.

Little, L. 1991. *Learner Autonomy1. Definitions, Issues, and Problem.* Dublin: Authentik.

O'Rourke, B. / Carson, L. (eds). 2010. *Language Learner Autonomy – Policy, Curriculum, Classroom. A Festschrift in Honour of David Little.* Oxford: Peter Lang.

Page, B. (ed). 1992. *Letting Go, Taking Hold.* London: CILT.

Wolff, D. 2003. Content and language integrated learning: a framework for the development of learner autonomy. In D. Little/ J. Ridley/ E. Ushioda (eds). *Learner Autonomy in the Foreign Language Classroom: Teacher, Learner, Curriculum and Assessment.* Dublin: Authentik, 211 – 222.

Wolff, D. 2011. CLIL and Learner Autonomy: relating two educational concepts. *Education et Societés Plurilingues,* 30/6, 69–80.

SUSANA NICOLAS

# Introduction

Content and Language Integrated Learning (CLIL) has transformed the educational scene and brought about a revolution of teaching methods and principles in the bilingual education environment. The major challenge in the implementation of a teacher education curriculum in CLIL is the integration of different teaching approaches to promote content and language mastery. What is certain is that there is no fixed model for CLIL and that for resources to be effective they have to be contextualized and motivating for both teachers and students. The four Cs (Content, Cognition, Communication and Culture) proposed by Coyle (1999) as framework for CLIL implementations find in drama a powerful meeting point to develop communicative skills and beyond. CLIL opens new possibilities for the implementation of drama in its multiple varieties: role-play, simulations, drama activities, educational drama and so on. The versatility of bilingual education enables teachers to adopt a more holistic and inclusive approach to classroom practice. This book proposes articles on the possibilities of drama as a challenging learning experience from primary to higher education.

Susan Hillyard's chapter looks at both Drama and CLIL as motivating forces in the English language classroom and analyses the relationship between the two approaches. She analyses the relationship between thinking skills development through Process Drama and highlights specific models explored within a global context. Practical activities, essential to drama, are shown to fit into a number of CLIL dimensions, intrinsically embedded in the drama experience, and, therefore, leading to more effective language acquisition.

Kemal Sinan Ozmen and Cem Balnikali discuss the theory and practice of integrating theatre acting theories to pre-service English teacher education. In this chapter, in addition to a current review of this field, specific practical tasks and suggestions are offered to teacher educators with no acting background but with the motivation to promote a strong pedagogical variety and diversity for their student teachers.

Tomas Motos and Donna Lee's chapter proposes Playback Theatre as the clear embodiment of CLIL methodology. They introduce an explanation and discussion of Playback Theatre, the components and processes involved in a PT session, and the areas where it is used, all with a special focus on education. They show two specific examples of the use of this theatrical format, firstly with an adult audience, and secondly with high school students, demonstrating the importance of PT in the practice of mediation. Finally, the authors present PT as an optimal application of the CLL methodology for the development and promotion of interactive, communicative and creative key skills.

Patricia Martín presents a workshop devoted to the Arts and Crafts subject through the Mantle of the Expert technique. Starting with a children book, *Katie Morag and the Wedding* by Mairi Hedderwick, She develops the complete outline of the activity and the final performance in class. The strategies of this technique are displayed looking at the teacher-in-role function and the creation of the plot by the students. Different activity corners were created in order to manage a group of thirty pupils performing roles in various scenarios. Creativity is encouraged all the time as the main objective. The atmosphere of 'reality' inherent in all Mantle of the Expert experiences provides also the opportunity to develop communicative competence and meaningful learning.

Nailya Garipova's chapter proposes bilingual context plays starting from the reality of the pupils today enabling teachers easier access to adopt a communicative approach in the foreign language teaching according to the CLIL methodology. The successful performance of the works analyzed throughout this article highlights the real need for a different approach in a foreign language teaching. The chapter shows how bilingual context plays encourage participation and communication between pupils from different nationalities and enhance their cooperation and tolerance.

The final chapter aims at presenting Readers' Theatre as a useful tool in the CLIL classroom to pursue not only language aims, but also educational goals. Through the discussion of its benefits and pitfalls, Raquel Fernández justifies the use of RT in CLIL classrooms, taking its potential advantages as the starting point and supporting its use further by connecting it with the 4 Cs stated by Do Coyle. She concludes with a set of didactic guidelines and steps for further researchers interested in studying the use of RT and those practitioners willing to implement it in their classrooms.

Susan Hillyard[1]

# Drama and CLIL: The power of connection

## Introduction

This chapter regards both Drama and CLIL as motivating forces in the English language classroom and analyses the relationship between the two approaches. Both are defined for the purposes of this paper. The five dimensions of CLIL are analysed through the eyes of Drama as not only a content subject in itself but also as an appropriate CLIL technique. Practical activities, essential to Drama, are shown to fit into a number of the dimensions of CLIL and are intrinsically embedded in the Drama experience, leading to more effective language acquisition. Not only do both approaches motivate students through engagement and connection, but they are also connected in their holistic nature, engaging the whole learner in the learning process. The word 'connection' in the title thus refers to the connection between the two disciplines and to the way in which both act as motivating forces for students in language classrooms by helping them to make the connections they need between their real lives and classroom life.

## As English moves from foreign language to basic skill

According to Graddol as "global English makes the transition from 'foreign language' to basic skill" (2006:6), a new world English language

---

1    Some of this material was previously presented in "Drama and CLIL: The Power of Connection", *Humanity Language Teaching*, 12 (2010) <www.hltm ag.co.uk/dec10/sart10.rtf>.

project will take shape and CLIL may well be part of that trend. He sees global English as an innovation which follows innovation diffusion theory and which will be taken up in different ways, through different means, at different rates and with different measures of success. He cites CLIL as "a significant curriculum trend in Europe" (2006: 8) and admits that similar approaches are now used under different names in many countries.

The interesting issue is to tie together all the approaches and to find out what works best and where, according to the experiences of each context. It is not necessarily a straightforward task. Marsland (1998) indicates that CLIL is sometimes regarded in Finland rather too simply as just 'Teaching Content through English' whereas Content and Language Integrated Learning is really a sophisticated and multi-faceted educational approach. Hellekjaer, (1999) agreeing with Marsland also claims that experience shows that more than just 'comprehensible input' is needed to attain competent levels in learners. The Canadian researcher Merril Swain claims that 'comprehensible output', the opportunity to use the target language for demanding oral and written tasks, is just as necessary and it is here where Drama can play a very relevant part, since it is the production of meaningful language, both body and verbal, in as near as possible real life contexts that is the essence of Drama.

Thus it is that I propose that the question of connection, vital to real learning, can be addressed through approaches envisioned within the five dimensions and foci of Drama and of the CLIL compendium.

## The question of motivation as a crucial factor in the classroom

It has long been felt that motivation may be an important factor in the acquisition of a foreign or second language and with the 'World English Project' as suggested by Graddol (2006) the issue may even become crucial to successful EL teaching and learning. However much we discuss its importance it is not always easy to pin down what motivation actually is. Dörnyei pertinently quotes Martin Covington on this point: "Motivation, like the concept of gravity, is easier to describe (in terms of its outward, observable effects) than it is to define" (2001: 7).

Certainly, it is easier to describe the outward signs as we have all registered them in their positive aspects and their negative aspects in countless classrooms all over the world. Not only this, but the outward signs of, for example, always doing homework on time and arriving early and eager to be in class, compared with finding the lesson boring and complaining about it, affect classroom dynamics. Individual and group responses lead to successful or unsuccessful classroom practices, no matter how diligent and experienced the individual teacher might be.

It has always been my contention, as an educational dramatist, that Drama is a motivational force in the classroom, particularly in language classrooms. Due to its essentially holistic approach to the learners' needs, Drama appeals to all students, no matter their learning style, and regains the often lost playfulness of younger learners. It employs practical, near to real-life role plays, developing comprehensible output on the part of the students, deploying collaborative techniques, and exercising thinking skills, often through problem solving tasks and practising conflict resolution. It is true learning by doing. It might be the nearest many students get to a real life/ first hand experience in school.

We are all cognizant with the theory of intrinsic or extrinsic motivation, with Maslow's pyramid, and perhaps also with Jarvis' theory of learning and Cambourne's model of the Whole Language Approach, not to mention Cummins and Fisher, yet the concrete control of motivational aspects still eludes us in practice. Dörnyei steers clear of trying to pin it down concisely by saying that motivation is:

> an abstract concept that we use to explain why people think and behave as they do. It is obvious that in this sense the term subsumes a whole range of motives – from financial incentives such as a raise in salary to idealistic beliefs such as the desire for freedom – that have very little in common except that they influence behaviour. Thus, 'motivation' is best seen as a broad umbrella term that covers a variety of meanings (2001: 1).

More recently, Dornyei (2013) has developed a number of theories to relate them to SLA, making a strong relationship between identity and motivation. He has developed a tripartite theory:

a)   The Ideal L2 Self, which concerns the L2-specific facet of one's ideal self: if the person we would like to become speaks an L2
b)   The Ought-to L2 Self, which concerns the attributes that individuals believe they ought to possess to avoid possible negative outcomes.
c)   The L2 Learning Experience, which concerns situation-specific motives related to the immediate learning environment and experience.

Maintaining that if the person, in our imagination, that we would like to become, speaks an L2, the *ideal L2 self* and the *ought to L2 self* combined with enjoying the learning experience also act as powerful motivators to learn the L2 (2013: 2–3). Not only does CLIL support this kind of analysis in its emphasis on learning to learn but Drama actually promotes personal development in this field through the use of role play and the mask of 'the other'.

## Motivation through connection

We need to harness the force of this motivation magnet to make the best use of the restricted amount of time we usually have in the EFL classroom. To do this, it may be more profitable to see motivation as *connection* or *engagement* and try to develop our own theory from the daily lived lives of our experiences within the classroom itself. This connection relates to any relationship in real life and is crucial to the desire to "stay beside", to "spend time with", to "inhabit", or to the notion of tacit knowledge (Polanyi, 1958) where one "lives IN the skills, or where one indwells only that to which one is committed; it has to do with passion". Ian Tudor in his article in *HLT*, Pilgrims Magazine, (Jan 2004), says that connection "involves students discovering a sense of personal meaningfulness in their language learning in one way or another". Again, this is extremely abstract, but clearly obvious if it is seen through the holistic lens of the CLIL approach and Educational Drama teaching frames.

## A definition of Drama

The definition of Drama used here is very broad and is more related to such terms as Educational Drama, Applied Drama and Process Drama, all pedagogical tools derived from theatre techniques. It is the enactment of real and imagined events through role play, improvisation, or play-making and uses the speaking body in the empty space to enable individuals and groups to explore, shape and represent the human condition in symbolic, metaphorical or dramatic form. In the words of the DICE report it is concerned with "using dramatic art to connect thought and feeling so that young people can explore and reflect subject matter, test and try out new ideas, acquire new knowledge, create new values, and build self-efficacy and self-esteem [...] It derives from the Greek word Dran – to do. Drama is something of significance that is 'done' or enacted. It is action explored in time and space" (http://www.dramanetwo rk.eu/).

## How Drama is used in the classroom

It is important to stress that Drama is not the same as Theatre which involves the reading of scripts and plays, written by a playwright, the academic study of characters and their interpretation through acting on a stage in front of an audience. Theatre always has a Director and a Stage Manager. This type of work includes the production of a school play or the end- of -year school concert with lighting, costumes, make up and sound effects all rehearsed and repeated over a long period of time. It often implies the director holding auditions and selecting a small elite of talented students. Drama, on the other hand, does not discriminate; it is for everybody.

Through the quotations below I sum up how Drama relates to the teacher's work in the classroom. These quotations are adapted from Heathcote's work (1984):

| **Teacher** |
|:---:|
| One who creates learning situations for others. A person whose energies and skills are at the service, during the professional situation of the pupils. Not one who tries to give away her knowledge to someone else. |

| **Education** |
|:---:|
| The moment whereby all the understanding you had before is sharpened into a new juxtaposition, because of what you have DONE. |

| **Drama** |
|:---:|
| Anything which involves people in active role-taking situations in which attitudes, not characters, are the chief concern, lived at life-rate (that is discovery at this moment, not memory-based) and obeying the natural laws of the medium:<br>- a willing suspension of disbelief<br>- agreement to pretence<br>- employing all past experiences<br>- employing any conjecture of imagination<br>to create a living, moving picture of life which aims at surprise and discovery for the participants rather than for any onlookers. |

| **Theatre** |
|:---:|
| The work of writing, producing and acting in plays where specialist actors rehearse a script for a given period of time, following the director's instructions with the aim of pleasing and entertaining or educating an audience. It is a pure art form. |

Figure 1.1. Some drama concepts.

Drama takes language and content and transforms it from the written, viewed or heard word into action. It makes itself a learning medium where the student becomes the doer of the language, taking risks to both understand and produce. It uses the body, the mind, the soul in combination where the student becomes the protagonist of the speech act and actually experiences something of the role of the real or the imagined speaker. It comes in many shapes and sizes such as language games, role play, improvisation, puppet plays, mask making and using, mime, movement, performance poetry, radio plays, singing action songs, chanting, dancing and any other mode which uses the faculties of the human body to express meaning.

Drama has developed over the years to be seen by some education authorities as an efficient learning medium for all levels, ages, abilities and subjects. It is holistic and polysemic in nature and therefore uses all the channels of the learner rendering their learning deeper and more substantial. Neelands and Goode (2006) explain as many as seventy two conventions of which around twenty are considered to be the most popular (explained below) and it is from this great wealth of classroom applications that the skilled Drama and CLIL teacher can draw.

## A definition of CLIL

There are as many definitions of CLIL as there are CLIL teachers and contexts. We all know that the concept of CLIL is not new but the label is indeed new, having been coined by David Marsh from the University of Jyväskylä in Finland in 1994, and once something has a label then it takes on new dimensions. Even as long ago as 1975 when the Bullock Report, *A Language for Life*, was published in England the connection between content and language was mooted. What Bullock said, in a nutshell, was that all content teachers had to be language teachers and as a corollary, it could be added that all language teachers had to be content teachers. The principal recommendations stated: "Each school should have an organized policy for language across the curriculum, establishing every teacher's involvement in language and reading development throughout the years of schooling" (1975: 137–139; 190; 89; 171).

Of course, there was not such a call for foreign language teaching in those days. It was a matter of raising the level of language development in first language English speakers. The label now, however, allows the concept to be discussed in a variety of contexts. Each teacher can examine how the basic idea can be adapted, if indeed at all, to a new and different context from the one in which it was born. Perhaps most interesting is that the spread and shift of the English language throughout the globalised world, at such an exponential rate, has prompted stakeholders to question, analyse, compare, contrast and discuss just where we are heading and what the acronym CLIL actually means. For the purposes of this chapter I shall define it as an approach where school or university subjects are taught through the medium of a foreign or second language when both the contents and the language play a joint and equal role.

## How CLIL is used in the classroom

Just as Drama has its own set of conventions, so too does CLIL. It concerns itself, depending on the context, with teaching a language in an integrated way through the five skills of that language: listening, speaking, reading, writing and thinking and it does it by applying a multitude of conventions designed to have the students DOING the activities rather than listening to the teacher. It employs the watch/read/listen then DO genre and relates specifically to the development of the HOTS (higher order thinking skills) of Bloom's taxonomy such as analyse, evaluate and create, rather than stressing only the lower order thinking skills or the LOTS (lower order thinking skills), such as remember, understand, apply.

CLIL also develops different but interconnected thinking skills such as creative, logical, reasoning, quantitative, qualitative, and lateral thinking skills through the techniques and activities that the students actually perform either as individuals or in groups. It also stresses metacognition and training students in learning to learn. These skills are required by the new digital, 21st century learner. Again the motivational aspects of CLIL are easy to understand as, once again, the student becomes the protagonist and the teacher a facilitator of learning situations instead of a transmitter of information. Such conventions as visual organisers/graphic organisers and aids such as diagrams and charts are used to help learners remember new information by making thinking visual.

They involve writing down or drawing ideas and making connections. Organisers can be simple or complex, but all of them have connecting parts.

## Conventions: The five dimensions of Drama

Drama may be said to be composed of five dimensions under the acronym SPICE, all defining developmental processes within the growing person:

SOCIAL development
PHYSICAL development
INTELLECTUAL development
CREATIVE development and
EMOTIONAL development.

It is not to be confused with theatre as it is not prescribed by an author or a director but is used for educational purposes rather than for entertainment. It fits well into any education system and, in my experience, into developing language acquisition in a more natural way than traditional ways in ELT

## Conventions: The five dimensions of CLIL

CLIL's original five dimensions are summarised thus through the TIXes:

ENTIX – dealing with the environment
CONTIX – the content or subject matter
LANTIX – the English language dimension
LEARNTIX – awareness of "Learning to Learn", or learner training.
CULTIX – dealing with culture and intercultural communication and understanding

I will endeavour to show how the combination of both Drama and CLIL components can act as a compelling force for teachers to become part of this global movement in keeping our young learners motivated to become competent bilinguals.


## Connecting Drama and CLIL


The five dimensions of CLIL and the five dimensions of Drama show clearly how both are motivating approaches for ELT practitioners and their students. Both are the almost perfect holistic and humanistic approaches to language acquisition in that they deal with the whole person in the big picture of life itself – not only in life in general, but life in a globalised world where Ministries of Education are making huge reforms.

Both approaches have certain tenets at their core although they concentrate on differing areas of the teaching and learning process. Drama approaches tend to concentrate on the growing person while CLIL approaches relate more to the learning itself. Both are complex and holistic in nature and feed into and from each other if viewed as parallel as in the chart below. Both Drama and CLIL promote connection because the fundamental philosophy is holistic and appeals to the needs of young learners. The five 'tixes' of CLIL overlap, intertwine, and weave their way through the minds, the souls and the bodies of the students in the charge of teachers worldwide. The Drama elements appeal to the human condition and the needs of learners to grow and develop in all five areas. CLIL may be considered a sophisticated extension of TBL (Task Based Learning), of project work, of LAC (Language Across the Curriculum), of bilingual immersion, of EIL (English as an International Language), of EGL (English as a Global Language). Without a doubt, for those who wish to move into a more global role as a teacher of EFL, Drama combined with CLIL can be a solution.

CLIL deals with subject areas or content which can sometimes be dry and technical, even when practised by an experienced teacher. Drama can move that content into the affective and physical areas so necessary for many young learners to find it at least meaningful. In comparing the two approaches it becomes clear that Drama behaves in a way which fits snugly into the CLIL dimensions as can be outlined in the chart below.

| CLIL Component | Drama |
|---|---|
| Cultix<br>Culture | Embedded.<br>Exploring other cultures/habits/behaviours/ stereotypes |
| Learntix<br>Learning | Embedded<br>Reflection /thinking skills esp. critical/creative/ analytical<br>/interpretative/ metacognition/<br>learning to learn |
| Entix<br>Environment | Embedded.<br>Exploring global issues/ environmental problems<br>Creating an artistic environment for all in schools/ institutions |
| Contix<br>Content | Embedded.<br>Literature of Drama/Stories<br>Cross Curricular e.g. History, Science<br>Mantle of the Expert |
| Lantix<br>Language | Embedded.<br>ESP through role play<br>Conversation/negotiation/<br>functions/ register/pronunciation/<br>modulation/diction |
| Engagement | Embedded.<br>Personal experience/imagined experience/play/<br>SPICE/self exploration and development. |
| Learning Outcomes | Embedded.<br>Scaffolding<br>Comprehensible OUTPUT<br>Published in the public forum of production ( written, spoken, web) |

Figure 1.2. Comparison of CLIL Component and Drama Forms.

# A comparison of thinking within the discipline of Drama and in CLIL

Einstein saw more than a century ago the important link between the imagination and thinking. If students can be encouraged to imagine, they can begin to change their perceptions and understand that there are other ways of thinking from their own boxes of culturally transmitted values and norms. Thus, they can begin to think in an intercultural manner and also understand the societal processes at work in their understanding of their own identity and eventually that of others. This also contributes to citizenship and exploring community values.

## Educational Drama and thinking skills

| High quality thinking | *High quality drama* |
|---|---|
| It is not routine – the path of action is not fully known in advance | *Drama is not just re-enactment of what is known. The children make decisions that influence the direction of the drama and they are given ownership, with their ideas being used to develop the drama.* |
| It tends to be complex – the total path is not visible from a single viewpoint | *Drama explores through role, the same situation from the viewpoints of different characters. It is not a linear process.* |
| It yields multiple rather than unique solutions | *Drama is "open". Scenes can be reworked and re-played in many ways with a multiplicity of solutions and outcomes.* |
| It involves nuanced judgment and interpretation | *Nuance is key to drama. Meanings are arrived at and communicated in a variety of ways, verbal, visual and kinaesthetic. Each person in an audience and each participant in the drama will interpret the drama somewhat differently, depending on their present understandings and experience.* |

| High quality thinking | *High quality drama* |
|---|---|
| It can involve the application of multiple criteria which may conflict with one another | *Drama involves problem solving and the resolution of dilemmas both within the drama and in the process of making the drama.* |
| It involves uncertainty – not everything about the task at hand is known | *Drama in education develops. It cannot be known what will emerge in the process as it is interactive and dynamic by nature. It is not about re-enacting what is known and certain, but about discovering and exploring what is uncertain.* |
| It involves imposing meaning – finding structure in apparent disorder | *Drama is all about finding, making and communicating meanings. It is structured, mainly by the teacher initially, but as children become more experienced and develop their drama skills they are more able to take over responsibility for structuring their own drama and communicating meaning to others through performance.* |
| It is effortful – considerable mental work is needed for the kinds of elaboration and judgements required | *Good drama is an active and interactive experience, which is both intellectually and emotionally demanding for both participants and audience.* |

Figure 1.3. A comparison of thinking skills and Drama.

Note. Right hand column: *Baldwin P. Chair National Drama from Keynote Speech National Drama Conference in Edinburgh (April 2002).*
Left Hand column*: Classrooms: a review and evaluation of approaches for developing pupils' thinking" Dr Carol McGuinness, Queen's University, Belfast, Crown Copyright, HMSO, 1999 (ISBN 1 84185 013 6).*

# Drama conventions suitable for CLIL classrooms

Superficially it may seem that Drama conventions cannot fit with subject classrooms although this was proved to be untrue, particularly during the 60s and 70s in the UK , when Drama was used extensively in infant, primary and secondary classrooms particularly in the teaching of Literature, Maths, Sciences and Social Sciences. Imaginative teachers were able to transform the dry facts and figures into a living, moving re-enactment using the whole person within the present moment so that all the channels of learning came into effect. Subject classrooms were transformed into experiential artistic laboratories where concepts, previously dead on the page, began to stand up and live.

In primary classrooms it is particularly easy to turn the digestive system or the rain cycle or the planetary system or atoms and molecules into living representations of such concepts through improvisation (see N° 1 in the selected conventions below), role play, hot seating (N° 10) and mime and movement. Likewise, any historical period, event or figure can come to life by standing up the text through those same conventions and others such as soundscape (N° 16) and role on the wall (N° 13), meetings (N° 8), trials (N° 9), interviews (N° 11), thought tracking (N° 4), eavesdropping (N° 21), decision alley (N° 17), stranger in role (N° 2 – variation), tableau (N° 3), freeze frame (N° 3- variation) and if this is combined with Teacher in Role (N° 2) then it becomes even more compelling.

Even for University students at Masters level who are studying a content subject e.g. Chemistry, Economics, Management, Physics etc. through a foreign language, such conventions as the interview (TV or Radio) (N° 11), meetings (N° 8), writing in role, (N° 7) mapping (N° 6), a trial (N° 9), a ceremony (N° 12), Forum Theatre ( N° 23) and Mantle of the Expert (N° 25) can be used to effect. In almost all subjects, conventions such as Narration (N° 5) and Discussion (N°24) can be used to enhance and deepen comprehension and productive expression. Such changes in classroom dynamics lead to personal development and therefore motivation for the students and professional development for the teacher as she has to re-think her role and her style within the classroom itself. These conventions often require few resources as they use "the speaking body in the empty space" concept. The main requirement is that the teachers are trained in this methodology.

## Some useful process Drama conventions (a selection)

1.  *Improvisation:* Unscripted, unrehearsed scene, co-created spon-
    taneously, and not written down before being presenting. It may
    be a whole-group scene (such as a crowd scene at the market-
    place), or students may work in pairs and/or small groups, with
    all groups exploring the same theme/roles simultaneously (such
    as a family at the dinner table, where the parents intend to an-
    nounce their plans to get a divorce). In whole-group scenes, the
    teacher also may take a role (see convention N° 2, below).

2.  *Teacher in Role (TIR):* The teacher takes on the role of a charac-
    ter within the drama. In any given drama, the teacher may take a
    number of different roles. Example: The teacher initiates the dra-
    ma by taking the role of a messenger, coming to warn a group of
    townspeople about a plague coming to their town. Later, he/she
    takes the role of the Mayor; later another role within the drama.

    The most effective roles tend to be mid-status roles (i.e.,
    a messenger from the king, rather than either the king himself
    or simply one of his subjects, along with the students.) Effective
    roles for the teacher will also project an obvious attitude toward
    the event taking place – curiosity, disdain, concern, disapprov-
    al, excitement, opposition, etc. TIR serves many essential func-
    tions, including helping students stay in role, building interest
    in and commitment to the unfolding drama, providing needed
    information from within the drama, and/or steering the drama
    in a particular direction without reverting to teacher-in-front-of-
    the-class mode.

* Variation: *Stranger in Role* – A friend or colleague of the teacher
appears in costume as a particular character within the drama. He/she
remains silent as long as possible, waiting for the students to draw him/
her out, define his/her character, and discover their own characters'
relationships to that character.

3.  *Tableau (Still Image):* In a small group, students position them-
    selves to create a picture expressing the essence of a certain situ-
    ation, idea, or dynamic. (It helps to set a time limit, e.g., counting

backwards from ten, then saying, 'Freeze') Tableaux can be followed up with Thought-Tracking (see N° 4) to help students extract meaning from the image and practice speaking.

\* Variation: *Freeze-Frame* – A series of Still Images depicting an important event within a drama or a work of literature, from history, etc.

Example: Cinderella cleaning for her stepmother and stepsisters; Cinderella helping them get ready to go to the ball; Cinderella daydreaming about going to the ball; the appearance of the Fairy Godmother.

4.  *Thought-Tracking:* The teacher freezes the drama (or it's already frozen, as in Tableaux) and taps each actor on the shoulder, one at a time, prompting him/her to speak aloud the character's private feelings and/or thoughts, or to answer a question in character.

5.  *Narration:* Teacher narrates part of a story, while students either…
    1) listen (usually with eyes closed), or
    2) pantomime the actions.

Example: Teacher narrates, while students pantomime: "The girl wakes up. She puts on the magic hat. She goes outside. She sits in the garden. She…"
    Narration is a very effective way of beginning a drama, moving it forward, creating atmosphere, providing needed information, focusing distracted students, encouraging reflection, or maintaining control of an unruly group of students.

\* Variation: *Guided Tour* – A form of narration that provides the group with a detailed mental picture of the environment in which the drama is to take place.

6.  *Mapping:* The teacher elicits from the class, together as a whole group, the information and details needed to create a map or floor-plan of an important area in the drama story, such as the village where everything takes place or the scene of a crime. Excellent means for establishing a collective sense of place.

\* Variation: Small groups make individual maps showing contextual details or depicting their ideal visions for particular sites within the drama story.

Example: In a drama involving a school, students draw a birds-eye-view of their ideal campus, indicating the buildings, recreational facilities, grassy areas, etc.

7. *Writing in Role:* In role as characters in the drama, students write reflectively about a particular event or dynamic in the drama. They may write journal entries, poems, letters or messages to other characters in the drama, etc. Excellent tool for stimulating student reflection and student practice of L2 writing skills, and also for aiding the teacher in assessing student comprehension.

8. *Meetings:*
   1) Whole class meeting, in which the teacher in role either imparts important information to the students in role, or gathers it from them.

Example: The teacher in role as a private investigator asks questions of community members about a missing person.

   2) Small group meetings (or whole class meetings, if class is small), in which the students in role may suggest strategies, plan future action, solve problems, etc.

Example: Prisoners of war meet to determine how they will escape their captors.

9. *Trials:* One or more people in role are interrogated (as in N° 10, Hot Seating) by the other students in role as committee members, examiners, jurors, or the like, with teacher in role as committee chair or similar role.

10. *Hot-Seating:* A group of students questions one or more people in role to gather information about his/her/their identity, prior actions, or motivations; an event that he/she/they witnessed, etc.

Example 1: During a trial or a meeting (conventions N° 8 & 9), students in role as members of a committee interrogate someone in role who claims to have committed (or not committed) a particular action. The committee seeks to determine the truth and/or the motivation behind his/her action.

Example 2: To begin a drama, the teacher sits before the class in role as Copernicus, and students ask him questions about his life.

11.   *Interview:* Students act as newspaper reporters, gathering information about a scene. This can either be done in pairs or small groups, each with one or two reporters and one or more interviewees, or as a whole-group press conference with the interviewee(s) in the Hot Seat (convention N° 10).

12.   *Ritual / Ceremony:* Small groups devise special events to mark, commemorate, or celebrate something of cultural or historical significance.

13.   *Role on the Wall:* The teacher draws a simple outline of a figure very big on a long sheet of butcher paper to represent a particular character from the unfolding drama. Inside the outlined figure, students write what they think the character might be thinking or feeling; around the outside of the figure they write what they think other characters in the drama might be thinking or feeling about that character, and/or their own thoughts or feelings about the character.

16.   *SoundScape:* Students use voice and/or percussion to suggest the sounds of a certain setting within a story.

* Variation: *DreamScape* – same, but suggesting a dreamt or imagined setting.

17.   *Decision Alley:* Students form two lines facing each other. One line agrees to favour one side of an issue; the other line agrees to favour the other. One student walks down the 'alley', while the students in the two lines take turns saying things to try to influence his/her opinion or decision. (First person in one line speaks, then first person in other line speaks, then second person in first line, etc.)

After 'walking the alley', the person announces his/her opinion or decision.

\* Variation: Each student peels away from the line-up and walks the alley in turn. Then everyone discusses the experience, enacted conversations and report them back to others.

23. *Forum Theatre:* One group of students enacts a scene. Observers may stop the drama any time to try to help the protagonist obtain his/her objectives via either replacing him/her or entering the scene as a new character.

24. *Reflective Discussion:* Out of role, in whole group or small groups, participants discuss what they did, saw, learned, thought, and/or felt.

25. *The Mantle of the Expert:* The student researches the expert and his discipline and his jargon and speaks through this mantle.

## Conclusions: the "new" paradigms of Drama and of CLIL

These methods require the teacher to comply with a number of approaches which are not necessarily routine in the EFL classroom nor in the subject classroom. Drama and CLIL principles come from a number of sources. As Steve Darn, Izmir University of Economics, Turkey (Teaching English BC) says "all teachers are teachers of language" (*The Bullock Report – A Language for Life*, 1975) to the wide-ranging advantages of cross-curricular bilingual teaching in statements from the *Content and Language Integrated Project* (CLIP). The benefits of CLIL may be seen in terms of cultural awareness, internationalization, language competence, preparation for life itself, study and working life, and, most crucially of all, increased motivation through the development of the person as a whole, not just a language learner. The advantage of putting CLIL together with Drama is that all of these elements are magnified producing a dynamic, effective and enjoyable learning experience for all.

From a language point of view, the CLIL 'approach' contains nothing new for the EL teacher except in opening up horizons and deepening the teacher's role in the general language learning process. CLIL aims to guide language processing and support language production in the same way as ELT, by teaching strategies for reading and listening and structures and lexis for spoken or written language. Combine it with Drama and it becomes even more powerful. What is different is that the language teacher is also the subject teacher, or that the subject teacher is also able to exploit opportunities for developing language skills. This is the essence of the CLIL teacher training issue.

Thus CLIL, combined with Drama, offers opportunities for real CLT and interactive communication between students and teachers, moving them forward into the World English Project where they can confidently take their place next to other non-native competent, knowledgeable, expressive English language speakers. Parker Palmer perhaps sums up my experience of using both Drama and CLIL approaches with students around the world.

> One student I heard about said she could not describe her good teachers because they were so different from each other. But she could describe her bad teachers because they were all the same: "Their words float somewhere in front of their faces, like the balloon speech in cartoons". With one remarkable image she said it all. Bad teachers distance themselves from the subject they are teaching–and, in the process, from their students. Good teachers join self, subject, and students in the fabric of life because they teach from an integral and undivided self; they manifest in their own lives, and evoke in their students, a "capacity for connectedness". They are able to weave a complex web of connections between themselves, their subjects, and their students, so that students can learn to weave a world for themselves (1997: 11).

# References

*Bloom's new taxonomy.* <http://tinyurl.com/k2qrftb> Accessed 5 June 2014.

*Bullock Report. A language for Life.* Report of the Committee of Enquiry appointed by the Secretary of State for Education and Science under the Chairmanship of Sir Alan Bullock FBA London: Her Majesty's Stationery Office 1975 © Crown copyright material is reproduced with the permission of the Controller of HMSO and the Queen's Printer for Scotland. <http://www.educationengland. org.uk/documents/bullock/bullock1975.html#01>. Accessed 30 May 2014.

Cambourne, B. 1993. *The Whole Story*. Australia: Scholastic Inc.

Covington, M. 1998. *The Will to Learn: A Guide for Motivating Young People*. Cambridge: Cambridge University Press.

*CLIL Compendium*. <http://apise.org.ar/apise/index.php?option=com_content&view=article&id=53&Itemid=77> Accessed 5 June 2014.

Cummins. J. 2001. *Negotiating Identities*. Los Angeles: California Association for Bilingual Education.

Darn, Steve. *CLILA European Overview*. <http://files.eric.ed.gov/fulltext/ED490775.pdf> Accessed 5 June 2014.

*DICE report on Educational Drama*. <http://www.dramanetwork.eu>. Accessed 30 May 2014.

Dörnyei, Z. / Chan, L. 2013. *Motivation and Vision: An Analysis of Future L2 Self Images, Sensory Styles, and Imagery Capacity Across Two Target Languages*. <http://www.zoltandornyei.co.uk/uploads/manuscript-proofs-with-corrections.pdf> Accessed 20 June 2014.

Fisher, R. 1990. *Teaching Children to Think*. Cornwall, England: T.J. Press.

Graddol, D. 2006. *English Next*. London: British Council. <http://www.britishcouncil.org/learning-research-englishnext.htm>. Accessed 5 June 2014.

____. 1997. *The Future of English*. London: British Council. <http://www.britishcouncil.org/learning-elt-research-papers.htm>. Accessed 5 June 2014.

Heathcote, D. / Johnson, L. / O'Neill, C. (eds). 1984. *Collected Writings on Education and Drama*. Illinois: Northwestern University Press.

Jarvis, P. 1992. *Paradoxes of Learning*. Josey Bass, San Francisco.

Marsland, David/ Hellekjaer, Ole. 1998, 1999. *Euroclic Bulletins 3 and 4*. <http://www.tieclil.org/html/links/EuroCLIC.html> Site under reconstruction.

Neelands, J. / Goode, T. 2006. *Structuring Drama Work*. Cambridge, UK: Cambridge University Press.

Palmer P. J. 1997. *The Courage to Teach: Exploring the Inner Land-scape of a Teacher's Life.* San Francisco: Josey-Bass. <http://www.couragerenewal.org/parker/writings/heart-of-a-teacher>. Accessed 20 June 2014.

Polyani, M. 2014. *Tacit Knowledge.* <http://infed.org/mobi/michael-polanyi-and-tacit-knowledge>. Accessed 5 June 2014.

Tudor, I. 2004. Towards a Methodology of Motivation. *Humanising Language teaching* 6/1. <http://www.hltmag.co.uk/jan04/mart2.htm>. Accessed 20 June 2014.

Tomás Motos Teruel / Donna Lee Fields

# Playback Theatre: Embodying the CLIL methodology

## Introduction

The simultaneous education of the mind and body, the nurturing of imagination, and the use of secular venues to foment education, has been the practice of dedicated teachers since time out of hand. However, during the 1800s, the insatiable desire of the Prussian royalty for absolute supremacy and compliant citizens, followed by the greed of factory owners during the Industrial Revolution who saw rote learning as the perfect venue to create mindless factory workers, derailed this more holistic pursuit, and fostered the advent of the autocratic classroom structure. Nowadays, as more and more educators eschew this autocratic educational model in favor of that which honors the individual student and caters to different learning styles, those didactic methodologies which foster the integration of content, stimulate an atmosphere of shared learning, and focus on elements which make education relevant to its audience, are becoming ever more in demand.

What we know today as Content Language Integrated Learning (CLIL) has been alive and well in the educational sphere since time out of hand, developed independently and informally by teachers who have considered issues deeply and who have worked at finding ways to reach out to their students when tried and true methods have failed. David Marsh saw the value of formalizing these independent practices, and dedicated himself to identifying the building blocks of a platform which would lead teachers and students to a more integrated style of teaching and learning. Through trial and error, insertion and clarification, CLIL has become a seamless patchwork of competencies and language acquisition, which outlines the theories, guidelines, and rational for the design of a student-centered classroom, which encourages creativity and the empowerment of the learners, and which insists on lessons steeped in authentic experiences.

The possibilities for the application of the methodology are infinite. Exploring the changing bio-systems of different countries in science classes, using modern architecture to study geometric shapes in engineering schools, visiting hospitals in medical studies, writing and sending job applications in vocational training courses, studying the billing history of thriving companies in economic classes – all of these are ways of applying the core features of CLIL to make learning more meaningful and personal. Nowhere, however, is the application more harmonious than in the theatre, and in particular that form known as Playback Theatre (PT). In this ingenious marriage of theatre, storytelling, and psychology, the precepts of CLIL are embodied to their fullest potential.

## What is Playback Theatre?

Playback Theatre is the spontaneous, instantaneous, and unscripted presentation of vignettes, performed in conventional and unconventional venues, working under the premise that the telling of oral stories is, in fact, an art form when presented with specifically delineated elements and when performed in interactive ways. This improvisational theatrical format strives to encourage dialogue and create connections between the audience and a corps of actors and musicians. Members of the audience volunteer to share personal stories which, filtered through ritual, theatrical aesthetics, dialogue, movement, and music, are immediately personified by the actors who give them artistic form. A "conductor" functions as an intermediary between the actors and the storyteller, gleaning the essence of the speaker's tale and verbalizing the core elements, with the intention of aiding the actors in augmenting their interpretations. The actors conscientiously present the stories with empathy and care, using humor to help generate perspective for the audience and the storyteller.

Playback Theatre was created by Jonathan Fox and his partner, Jo Salas, in the mid-1970s in a little town in the Hudson River Valley, about one hundred miles north of New York City (Fox, 1994; Fox, 1999; Fox & Dauber, 1999). Both educators, inspired by experimental theatre, psychodrama and the oral traditions of indigenous cultures, by Pedagogy of the Oppressed written by educator and theorist Paulo Freire, and Theatre of the Oppressed written by theatre practitioner Augusto Boal, spent several years testing and developing their theories and practices. Fox explains that their intention in establishing PT was to offer an intimate forum in which the audience neighbours, family or acquaintances could gather and share. "Many people have sad or dramatic stories that others are unaware or unwilling to listen to [in other venues]. I wanted Playback Theatre to be a place where everyone could tell their story and be heard" (Friedler: 2006). He also insists that if we, as a human race, are to actuate personal and social transformations, we need to listen to each other on a deeper level. As such, this art form creates a space for learning, healing, and creating bonds between people. Fox describes PT as a force to preserve the social ecology by "transforming the lives of people and forming groups" (1994: 12).

Early on, Fox and Salas decided to liberate the art form from conventional forums. It is largely due to this move to use the practice as a wider application and offering actuations in less conventional venues and audiences – that defines and has set PT apart from other theatrical forms. The first participants in this participatory theatrical experience were schoolchildren, the elderly and disabled, foster-home support groups, people undergoing rehabilitation, family therapy groups, and community action meetings, all in their own environments. Its success is credited, in part, to its format, its flexibility, the care and sensitivity with which the tales are treated, and its limitless possibilities.

PT is now regularly used in educational environments, in company improvement plans, in psychotherapy groups, in prisons, hospitals and at-risk youth centres, to name just a few of its venues. Its versatility of form helps in its proliferation as it can take place just as effectively in the conference rooms of a formal convention centre, as on a traditional stage, and any alternative space in between. Today, this therapeutic art form is gaining importance at an exponential rate. Not only is its global value universal, but it benefits from the universal truth that wherever there is a gathering of people – either planned or unplanned – there is always a story.

Rasa Friedler, founder and CEO of the SaludArte Foundation, an organization whose mission it is to demonstrate how the health of any given population can be directly affected by art and humour, explains that "PT is a major activator of the core potential of each person. It wakes up the best of what is dormant in every society and promotes integration amongst different artistic areas" (2006: 1). Today, this theatrical format is currently implemented in over 55 countries, helping tens of thousands of individuals and groups develop direct communication, and interconnect on an emotional level.

## *Components and the process of Playback Theatre*

From its earliest inception, the scope and purpose of PT was

> to reveal the form and meaning of any experience, even those that are ostensibly formless and ambiguous in the telling. [PT] dignifies stories with ritual and aesthetic awareness, and links them together so that they form a collective story about a community of people, whether this be a group of people whose lives are connected in an ongoing way, or one created in the moment such as that found in most public audiences…[PT] offers an arena in which the meaning of individual experience expands to become part of a shared sense of purposeful existence (1993: 22).

Fox emphasizes art, ritual and social interaction as the essential elements of PT (1999: 127). The relationship between these dimensions is interactive and over the course of any PT performance all three must be continually balanced. As the story unfolds, it is the domain of the conductor to weigh and adjust the tension in the dialectical flux of these three dimensions, leaving the actors to be free to measure the balance between the demands of their own performance and those of the social demands – of listening and being present (Salas, 2005).

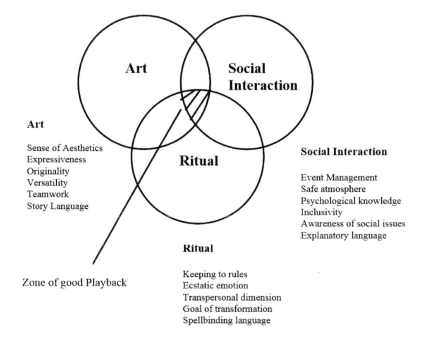

Figure 2.1. Essential elements of Playback Theatre. (Oivo: 6).

It is important to note that the element not given its fullest import in the above model is the fundamental role the participation of the audience has in the interaction; it is, in fact, of principal value and one of the underlying precepts of a 'good' enactment. (Dennis, 2004: 20).

The three defining elements:

(A)   the personal story (the content)
(B)   a ritual aesthetic (the form)
(C)   the context (locale)
are developed more fully below.

*A) The story*

Part of the intention of co-creators Fox and Salas in developing PT was to create and present a space in which every voice and any story could be heard, however ordinary or extraordinary, and in which any experience of life could be related, however frivolous or transcendent, comic or tragic. It is intended to be a platform upon which narrators can express their repressed emotions and be heard; they can relate experiences which, in any other forum they'd find difficult to share.

Through experience, Fox and Salas have deduced that, though spontaneity is one of the cornerstones of this art form, the process is most effective when the presentations revolve around a specific issue. For this reason, part of the ritual of PT includes involving the audience in choosing one theme which then serves as the impetus of each individual enactment. Narrators are encouraged to be guided by this chosen theme in chronicling their memories, fantasies, dreams, conflicts, and/ or feelings.

The following is an example of one session whose focus – selected by the audience – was on family relationships.

Antonio, a 25 year old man, related the following story, developed with the aid of the conductor:

| | |
|---|---|
| Antonio: | What do you think? Should I talk about friendships, girlfriend, or family? I have conflicts with everyone. |
| Conductor: | Whichever you want. |
| Antonio: | Well, the first one that comes to mind has to do with my sister and my mother. |
| Conductor: | What is your relationship with your mother? Can you describe her with two adjectives? |
| Antonio: | Well, my mother is a strong woman and extremely possessive. |
| Conductor: | And what is your sister like? |
| Antonio: | Very selfish. She's self-centred and has no empathy for anyone. |
| Conductor: | What is the story you'd like to tell? |
| Antonio: | Well, I want to be a pop singer. So, one morning my sister came home. She and my mother started talking |

about the gossip from the town. I was woken up by their voices, but I was afraid to leave my bedroom. When I finally did, both of them immediately started harping on me about my job situation. They said that I needed to look for a job, that I had to send out my CV... and a lot of other things. After that I told my sister that that night I was going to a competition for amateur singers. My sister sings also. When I sang the song I had written, she shot me down with: "Well, you don't have a good ear so why are you going to take part in the competition?"

The actors represented the above story and then the narrator was asked how he had viewed it as a whole. He responded that it was very well done and true to his narration. He felt that the actors captured the true spirit of his character and that of his sister. However, the mother was a bit exaggerated, as his mother in real life is more distracted. In any case, he did not take the option of asking the actors to redo any part of it, and left the stage very satisfied.


## B) The ritual

The aesthetic form of PT has a framework of expectations which can be considered ritualistic in a secular sense. This strict adherence to definitive steps honoured throughout the enactment, "symbolizes the repeated structures in space and time that provide stability and familiarity within which unpredictability can be found" (Salas, 2005: 117). Aside from defining the shape of the art form, this ritualized process facilitates interaction between the audience and the actors, and eases the former into partaking in the process; in other circumstances participants may not be so open or willing to expose themselves.

The physical arrangement of the venue is also considered part of PT's ritualistic structure, (though the corps of players can adapt the sessions to virtually any setting). The only requirement of the locale is that it has two defined areas: one for the actors and one for the audience (See Figure 2). In the area designated for the enactment of the stories (the stage), two chairs are placed to the side of the main arena. The chair closest to the audience is assigned to the conductor whose role it is to act as master of ceremonies, host, and companion to the narrator in the story-making process.

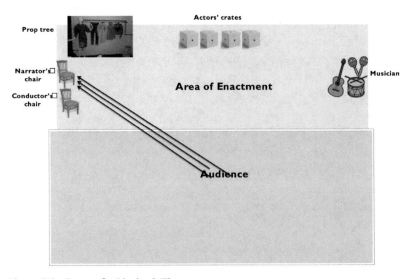

Figure 2.2. Setup of a Playback Theatre.

The second chair is for the narrator – a member of the audience who has volunteered to tell a personal story. Opposite the conductor is a musician who has at her/his disposition a variety of instruments. Towards the back of the stage, four or five chairs or crates are set up upon which the actors sit when they are not acting. These crates can also be used as props. On one side is a 'prop tree' draped in materials and various objects that can be used to embellish characters, indicate location, or symbolically represent other elements of the narration.

The following is a list of the 12 steps of the art form followed by a more detailed explanation of each:

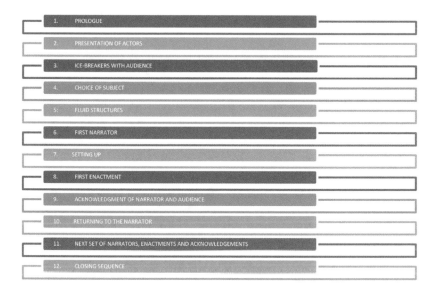

Figure 2.3. Structure of a Playback Theatre enactment.

1. *Prologue.* The musician infuses the setting with melodies and sounds. The conductor greets the audience and makes an introduction, explaining the structure of the event they have come to participate in, helping to establish a relationship between the corps of actors and the audience. The goal of this initial interaction is to create a warm and trusting environment in which each member of the audience feels heard, accepted and respected. As it is they who are the protagonists of the function, this is an essential step, as without the audience's willingness to share stories, there is no PT.

2. *Presentation of actors.* The conductor then gives the actors the floor, asking them to introduce themselves. One by one, they energetically enter the scene, give their names, and offering a short statement (1–2 sentences) either about something that happened to them recently or about a dominant feeling that they are experiencing at that moment. Following these introductions, the actors go to their crates (chairs) and take their seats.

3. *Ice-breaking games with audience.* The conductor proposes a game or a short exercise designed to relax the audience and to

create an atmosphere of trust and respect. The nature of the game is often related to the space chosen for the function.

4.   *Choosing the theme.* As mentioned above, PT sessions work best when the group is homogeneous and is focused on one specific topic of interest that has been agreed upon by the members of the audience. Though this template of conformity is the norm, equally viable are those sessions in which the stories of the narrators do not share a common thread.

5.   *Fluid Sculptures.* Before beginning the first narrative, the actors, musician and conductor give the viewers a demonstration of what they will experience by giving them an example of a possible interaction between the audience and the corps of players. This begins by the audience members, prompted by the conductor, communicate a sentiment; this feeling is then duly manifested by the actors and musicians using motion and sound. For instance, the conductor asks the group: 'How do you feel about coming to a PT performance for the first time?' A member of the audience raises a hand, the conductor thanks the person, requests the person's name, and then asks for a response. The person's response may be: 'I feel anxious' for which the conductor turns to the actors and repeats: 'This is Sue and she feels anxious'. The actors immediately construct a kind of sculpture with their bodies, which personifies anxiety. In this way the public sees that their participation will be received with 'respect and aesthetic attention' (Salas, 2005: 46). At the same time, they intuit that though their involvement is very welcome though they are under no obligation to participate.

6.   *First interview.* The conductor asks for a volunteer from the audience. An audience member steps forward and is then invited to take the seat on stage designated for the narrator. (The moment that this first participant moves from the audience to the stage is a defining and transitional moment for it breaches the theatre's traditional fourth wall.) The conductor then simultaneously attends to three branches of the enactment: the shaping of the story told by the narrator, the information necessary to incite the actors into movement, and the audience's reception of the tale portrayed by the actors. It is the conductor's job to filter through

the narration and identify key elements – how, what, when, and where the event happened, who was present, how it ended, and how the narrator felt in that situation – to help the actors identify the core features of the story.

When this part of the process is complete and the conductor feels that the actors have enough information to begin an enactment, the conductor invites the narrator to choose actors to play the primary and supporting characters. (One actor can represent more than one character.) The actor(s) selected stand up and prepare themselves for the scene while the conductor continues addressing questions to the narrator.

7.  *Setting up.* As the actors (silently) choose places on the stage to begin, the musician begins with tones and rhythm from different instruments to introduce the scene. The music at this time is an integral part of the ritual, serving a dual purpose of 1) creating an atmospheric setting, and 2) giving the actors more time to reflect on their assigned roles. As mentioned above, the crates these latter have been sitting on can be used and arranged in a variety of ways to help emphasize tone. In the same manner, the material and other objects hung on the 'props tree' can be utilized to help bring characters to life and to manifest symbolic themes.

8.  *Enactment.* The conductor now affects the transitory measures necessary to move from the narrative to the dramatic state – the enactment of the story. With the simple but dramatic phrase 'Let's watch!', indicating the change in role from passive 'citizens' listening to a narration, to co-creators in the transformational process, the actors and the musician take over. (Dennis, 2004: A10): the musician heightens the intensity of the music, the actors remove unnecessary props from the stage, and the conductor and narrator remain seated and watch with the rest of the audience members. From this point, the playes work together, presenting improvisational scenes which emphasize the essential events, and dilemmas, or conundrums, related by the narrator. As a rule, instead of placing an emphasis on linear structure, the scenes are more metaphoric than literal, the intention being to create a flow of moments without necessarily showing realistic details. What

is essential is that, at the heart of the performance, there exudes respect and understanding towards the narrator.

9.   *Acknowledgment.* When the actors feel that they have fleshed out the story as fully as possible, they regroup and acknowledge the narrator with a gesture which symbolizes their objective of offering their dramatization as a gift. This is an essential step in honouring both the person and the story.

10.  *Returning to the narrator.* With the actors still in position of homage, the conductor questions the narrator to ascertain whether the enactment has been true – if it has portrayed the fundamental idea of the tale. If the narrator is unsatisfied with any element of the performance the process continues: the conductor gleans more details from the storyteller, and asks the actors to interpret one or more parts of the story which will incorporate the clarifications. This replay is called 'correction'.

Occasionally, when a story has been accurately represented but the narrator is left confused, worried or distressed, the conductor may invite the actors to imagine and present an alternative ending. In the same vein, if the narrator herself requests a different outcome to the story, this new ending is called a 'transformation'.

At the completion of these enactments, the conductor thanks the narrator who is then invited to return to her/his seat in the audience.

11.  *New interviews, enactments and acknowledges.* A new audience member is invited to take the stage, and the process is repeated as often as time allows.

12.  *Closing sequence.* To emphasize the value the corpus of players place on the audience members, these former reprise echoes of the elements of the dramatic sequences that were created during the performance, in the form of four or five very short skits. Following this, the conductor thanks the audience for their participation and the musician plays a tune of farewell as the viewers leave their seats.

## The Context

In the hands of an experienced group of actors, PT is fluid and energetic and its effect magical; however, the structure of PT ignites change and discovery, and so, even those corps of players with little or no formal acting training will affect powerful results. Whether in prisons, at-risk youth centers, hospitals, or on the stage of a traditional theater, PT's fundamental framework is designed to help audiences search within themselves to resolve differences, to learn from the perspective of peers, and to make peace with their past.

As mentioned above, bringing the art form to an established community (instead of a group of audience members formed arbitrarily), is one of the key elements of PT. Offering an educational/therapeutic experience to participants in a familiar setting provides a shortcut in helping them become receptive to the process. It provides a door through which the audience can enter the participatory framework of the ritual and form of the art form. Aiding in establishing commitment to the process is a strong identification to the context; it helps weaken the resistance the audience might initially feel, and promotes a state of readiness, which gives the actors more direct access to the emotional threshold of the viewers.

Very often, Fox and Salas are asked about the importance of the level of experience of the players. Their answer is that enactments have been effective with actors of almost any skill level. The factor, which carries the most weight is that the players always act with respect and empathy, and are willing to be daring in the interpretation of the stories. In fact, so important are the elements of empathy and intuition in the interpretation that Salas cautions against enactments that do no more than produce superficial versions of stories narrated.

Not only the importance of experience but the very existence of a corps of actors in the process of PT has also been addressed – the question of whether or not the players are essential in reaching a sufficiently profound emotional level in the audience. Salas (2008) attests that when she began using PT in childcare centres, the children themselves filled the roles of both actors and spectators. The format was the same, as was the intention – to provide a therapeutic platform; however, the emphasis was on the process of breaking down barriers and helping the children listen to each other rather than on artistic competence. In relation to context, then, if the intention is to provide therapy to a community of audience members, the model, which eschews the participation of a professional corps of actors is viable and perhaps even recommended.

## Fields in which PT is practiced

Since its inception PT has been practised in many different fields and with several different purposes.

> ... [PT] is a versatile theatrical form that is equally at home in public theatres, schools, hospitals, residencies, corporate settings, conferences, and in forums for social change. It can be just as effective on the streets of southern India with Dalit people telling stories about police brutality, as in an outdoor community event exploring diversity in a small American town (Salas, 2009: 445).

Given its very nature PT conforms to the needs and concerns of every kind of audience and any environment. The versatility of the locales is reflected in articles published in *Interplay* (the quarterly review of the International Playback Theatre Network). These locales include cooperate offices (Hofman, 1997); prisons (Bett, 2000, Southard 2000); housing estates (Murphy, 2001); disability meetings (Day, 1998); mental health institutions (Muckley, 1998); youth centres (Wynter, 1998); refugee shelters (Robb, 2002); and indigenous communities (Cox, 1996).

### *In education*

PT is used in schools as a tool to help educators in their classrooms and to confront various issues that are traditionally difficult to resolve amongst many student bodies (Salas, 2005). The ways of adapting the format are infinite: as a way of presenting or reviewing material, PT can be used, for example, in a literature class. The students are given the opportunity to physically portray literary themes or historical characters. In a science class, groups of students can be asked to demonstrate the phases of the sun and cycles of the moon. In an art class, students can be challenged to represent primary, secondary and tertiary colours with their bodies and with materials taken from the prop tree. In higher education – in teacher training, for example – PT can be used as a way of encouraging the development of democratic participation in language and aesthetic education (Feldhendler, 2009). In social aspects of school such as with bullying, participants can relate their experiences and explore how they can all create a respectful and safe environment. In all of these modalities, the PT framework can be utilized either by professional actors or by the teachers and students (Wright, 2002).

*In social change*

As mentioned above, part of PT's missive is to open up pathways to produce constructive social interaction, to promote social justice, and to build community (Fox, 2007). Practitioners of the art form look for places where communication and coexistence are damaged by inequality and injustice. Their goal is to help individuals share their values and experiences while feeling supported by their neighbours, co-workers, or peers (Park- Fuller, 2003). Once these communities are identified, the players work with the members of a chosen community to find a space in which they can host the enactment. The cooperation between these two parties is an integral part of PT as it empowers the community to be part of the process and so be more invested in its resolution.

On a more global scale, PT has been used as the framework for forums in which victims of natural disasters, climate change, violence, or immigration issues, can share their experiences (Feldhendler, 2009). In the summer of 2008, for example, the Centre for Playback Theatre organised a program called 'After the Storm: Mobilizing Playback Theatre for Communities in Crisis' in New Orleans, the city which took the brunt of Hurricane Katrina which destroyed much of the city and its coast in 2005.

In relation to violence and immigration matters, PT players have gone into prisons and have interacted with inmates, helping them find methods of reconciliation, and have hosted sessions in immigration support groups in their host communities, aiding them in building bridges across cultural misunderstandings and language barriers (Barreto, 2008).

*In companies*

The theatre company has also successfully donned the role of supervisors and counsellors in a coaching format. Since the mid-1990s PT has most frequently been used as an effective ongoing training strategy on a variety of topics such as management and communication skills, and awareness of diversity (Stronks, 2013). In some cases, participants have described events that occur in the workplace on a regular basis which gave rise to conflicts or feelings of dissatisfaction. The actors represent the stories told and the conductor organizes a debate on the representation. In these sessions, participants later describe how they obtained valuable lessons from the process (Dennis, 2004).

*In psychotherapy, hospitals and mental health services*

Though not a therapeutic technique per se, PT does have therapeutic properties and can be adapted by specially trained therapists to use with their patients with excellent results. In a more general forum, participants obtain, among other benefits, self-awareness, opportunities for catharsis, connection with others and personal expression development (Salas, 2008). Presented always with an underlying lyrical and light touch, the process helps participants improve their self-esteem, promote relaxation, and connect with a greater sense of empathy (Moran and Allon, 2011). It has also been used in mental health services (Larkinson and Rowe, 2003).

## The harmony of Playback Theatre and CLIL methodology

One of PT's most valuable faces is as a straightforward educational tool to help students learn with the benefit of reaching all their varied learning styles that may not be addressed in the classroom. The traditional model is slowly being left behind and many teachers' intentions are to integrate lessons in all its senses – physically, philosophically, logistically – that are geared not towards rote memorization but rather to the different intelligences. This model is seen more and more as the appropriate and desired framework of curriculum dispersion in the educational setting. Formulized today under the acronym CLIL and championed by educators world-wide, this student-centered classroom is more a philosophy than a methodology. The classroom is not a space surrounded by immutable walls which house straight rows of desks isolated one from the other, facing an omnipotent and supposedly omniscient queen/king/managerial figure who lectures to submissive and passive students. Instead it is one in which everyone has equal value, and equal importance. The teacher serves as a facilitator and creates a forum within which the students work together to assimilate the information in their own way.

Yet, even though this structure and perspective towards education has gained a dedicated following, and the benefits are undeniable, there is still a dearth of materials and resources available for educators to pull from. The result is that most CLIL teachers have to create most of the materials themselves. This involves an enormous amount of work that is, even in the best circumstances, overwhelming for even the most dedicated. As a result, teachers desirous of new, meaningful and authentic ways of presenting curriculum, look for frameworks that they can use and adapt in order to animate their students. PT is tailored just for such inquiring educators.

The CLIL methodology is denoted in PT's very platform. The five elements that energize and bring a story to life in the theatre are: the body, the heart, the head, the context and creativity. First, one has to react with the body, next with the heart, and finally with reflection and knowledge (the head). The last element – the combination of reflection and knowledge, is enacted in a multicultural context, all in a creative environment (creativity) (Laferrière y Motos, 2003: 92), and so a teacher seeking to fit to find a forum which will accommodate the CLIL methodology into an educational forum, will find that the PT structure fits effortlessly into each identifier.

The relationship between the six CLIL core features and the essential PT elements, are elaborated below:

*Scaffolding,* credited as the key ingredient in helping students ease into a new subject, builds on a student's existing knowledge, skills, attitudes, interests and experience, fostering creative and critical thinking, and challenging students to advance (Mehisto: 2014). This corresponds to PT's method of beginning each session with different forms of ice-breaking techniques, and involving the audience in the choice of topics that will be subsequently developed throughout the enactment.

A *Safe and Enriching Environment* – using routine activities and discourse, guiding access to authentic learning materials – is reflected in PT's ritualistic approach to the artistic form, and of using personal stories from the audience members themselves.

*Active Learning*, synonymous with the balance of the interaction of the conductor and the rest of the participants in a PT event, the teacher acts as facilitator, while the stress during the lesson is on student involvement. A CLIL teacher's job is to inspire students to communicate, just as the conductor's role is to encourage the PT narrator to share; the students in a CLIL classroom are given the opportunity to take part in choosing the content of studies just as it is the PT narrator's choice of what story to share; the CLIL methodology encourages students to take part in the evaluative outcomes just as it is up to the narrator to assess the veracity of the enactment to the narrative. The CLIL teacher and the PT conductor share the distinction of being seemingly background players while being ultimately responsible for all the action and exchanges which occur during a class/enactment.

*Authenticity,* or the importance of maximizing students' interests in any subject and making regular connections to students' lives, is featured in the instance of using real stories from the audience members.

*Multiple Focus,* or the importance of integrating several subjects and reflecting on the learning process, is reflected in the different narrations which are presented during the course of any enactment, plus the opportunity PT gives to the narrator to reflect on whether unexpected issues were resolved during the enactment and whether others had been resolved.

*Cooperation* is the obvious component of the actors (students) working and learning together.

# Linguistic elements of PT and CLIL methodology

The beauty of the CLIL methodology is its versatility and its focus not necessarily on language but on the verbal expression of content – in any language – and the importance of permeating lessons with multi-cultural experiences. Although there are cases in theatre in which words are non-existent, such as in the behaviouristic mime experiment Act Without Words by Samuel Beckett, or in physical theatre, the spoken word is generally accepted as the key element in acting. Conceptually different from one culture to another, theatre can be perceived with a stress either on oral or visual senses. In native English-speaking countries, for instance, audiences are listeners by definition, whereas in Spanish-speaking countries, the stress is on the visual as an audience is called espectador (spectator). Among others, Jonathan Fox (1994), Jo Salas (2005), Daniel Feldhendler (2005, 2006 and 2009) and Janet Salas (2006) have written extensively on the relationship between PT and some aspects of verbal language.

The different linguistic roles within a PT group are relevant to the subsequent verbal expression and subliminal learning. Janet Salas (2006) delineates each member's role with the following distinctions:

| *Conductor* | • invites group members to tell stories<br>• interviews the narrator (asks questions, makes comments, asks for clarification, etc.)<br>• repeats, restates, summarises stories<br>• verbally guides, instructs, answers questions posed by actors |
|---|---|
| *Actor* | • listens and interprets conductor's interview and narrator's story<br>• listens actively and responds to other actors' stories, conversations and commentaries<br>• listens actively and responds to statements made during activities and forms such as the fluid sculptures, chorus, iconography (tableau), etc.<br>• listens actively and responds to dialogue and comments during scenes<br>• produces socially and culturally appropriate language |

| *Musician* | • hears and interprets conductor's interview and instructions, narrator's story, <br>• listens actively and responds to other actors' stories, conversations and commentaries <br>• listens actively and responds to comments made during activities, and forms such as fluid sculptures, chorus, iconography (tableau), etc. |
|---|---|
| *Narrator* | • relates a story, an experience, a dream, a memory, a fantasy, etc. <br>• listens and processes the conductor's questions <br>• understands the actors when they play the scene <br>• responds to/reflections on the enactment |
| *Actors' trainer/workshop leader* | • leads warm-up, trains corps of actors for activities, directs the flow of the session <br>• comments <br>• offers feedback <br>• directs reflection processes |
| *All participants* | • reflects verbally on their own and on the actions and performance of others <br>• interacts verbally in the group on a team and social level |

Table 2.1. Linguistic Role of Playback Theatre members.

The integration of content and verbal language is the core principle of CLIL methodology – the fluid exchange of language and content. The CLIL teacher creates occasions for the students to interact within the language as much as possible using curriculum content as the impetus. These linguistic opportunities are built in to the PT framework and the teacher need only follow the established steps set forth in the PT structure to be able to present an extraordinary environment in which students can practise and dramatically improve their linguistic skills.

There are, of course, certain linguistic elements which need to be at the students' disposal to ensure their ability to communicate in a foreign language. On a general scale, the students need to have learned the appropriate vocabulary in any given subject to be able to: describe, explain, evaluate, and draw conclusions. On a more specific note, students participating in a PT enactment need to be actively developing aural comprehension as much of their work is listening and interpreting stories from the narrator and receiving verbal cues from the conductor.

In the context of second-language learning, whether as a student participating in a classroom adaptation, or as a member of the corpus players, the effectiveness of PT has been proven to be overwhelmingly effective. Janet Salas (2006: 3–4), whose mother-tongue is English (New Zealand), is a teacher of German and EFL, and conducts a group of PT using German in their performances. As part of her ongoing analysis of the PT effectiveness, Salas collected her students' opinions on participating in PT in a second language, related to whether their experience helped their language learning or not. The following is one example: "The learning of the foreign language by doing PT is much more effective than learning with books or other methods. It is learning with all senses and emotions. When I, as a German speaker, trained for a PT enactment with an English-speaking (American) audience, it was such an intensive experience that that night I dreamt in English" (Salas, 2006: 4).

There are essentially two options in applying a second language in a PT enactment. The first is that the conductor and actors use their native language (L2) which would be the targeted language of study of the audience members (L2). The second possibility is that the actors and the conductor use L1, which would be the native language of the majority of the audience members, but not that of the corps of actors. A high level of concentration is necessary on the part of an audience which attends a function of PT in a second language (L2) to be able to understand the stories told and to follow the course of the drama. Salas lays out the necessary skills students would need in more detail (2006: 7).

The students would need to be able to:

- listen and understand not only the narration of the performances but also different accents, slang, idioms, etc.
- talk to strangers or acquaintances about personal matters
- speak in front of strangers
- participate in an interaction which includes comprehension of questions and the ability to respond appropriately.

Daniel Feldhendler, a professor of French at the Goethe University in Frankfurt, is considered one of the leading advocates and experts of

PT in L2 teaching. He considers PT as a practical and comprehensive approach to language training and as a tool for innovation in alternative methods of teaching and learning for both initial studies and advanced studies.

> Playback Theatre actively trains the skill of reflection as a mode of enhanced perception of self and others in communication. An integration of the underlying Playback skills which is a great significance in verbal communication takes place: active listening, hermeneutically deepened understanding of a message, transposing through a variety of modes of expression (body, voice, etc.), learning of appropriate verbal and non-verbal interactive response, dealing with feelings, learning as a transformative process and deepening of awareness, adoption of integrative feedback methods, building a pool of shared experience through process analysis, and perception of interpersonal and thematic connections (Feldhendler, (2007: 4).

Moreover, he states that conflict can be explored through the stories of the tellers and the group's life stories. He emphasizes that PT contains very useful tools for mediation and sensitization in multicultural and educational settings. The fact that the stories told are personal is an incomparable experience for the students as they are expressing things relevant to themselves and so, are empowered.

## Models of PT in the CLIL classroom

Theory aside, teachers need specifics and not just the framework when applying new methodology to their classrooms. It is the intention of the authors of this chapter, not only to present the theory of the symbiotic relationship between CLIL methodology and that of PT, but also to present concrete PT structures which CLIL teachers can use to adapt and apply in their classes. The following are two such examples[1]:

---

1       These lessons which mention 'different intelligences', refer to those multi-intelligences outlined in Howard Gardner's 'Theory of Multiple Intelligences', which are an integral part of a student-centered classroom.

*Social Sciences:*

- *The Narrator*: The teacher chooses student who is strong in linguistic intelligence.
- *Actors*: The teacher chooses four or five students who have demonstrated difficulties in the subject.
- *Conductor*: The teacher.
- *Musician*: A member of the student body with strong musical intelligence.
- *Prologue*: The teacher explains the format of the lesson.
- *Presentation of Actors*: The chosen four/five introduce themselves.
- *Ice-breaking games with audience*: The teacher (now the conductor) might ask the "audience" questions about a chapter that they have been studying, keeping the tone light, always with the intention of helping the students relax.
- *Choosing the theme*: The teacher can let the students choose the chapter/issue that they will elaborate on during the session. In this example, the students have chosen to focus on World War I.
- *Fluid Structure*: If the 'actors' are very comfortable with each other, the teacher ask them to enact this part of the process; if not, this step can be overlooked until such time as the teach is confident that no one will be uncomfortable in its attempt.
- *First Interview*: The 'conductor' asks the 'narrator' to speak about world leaders leading up to World War I and their role in the events that caused the war's outbreak. The 'actors' pay close attention in order to be able to personify one of these leaders and to know what to focus the dialogue on. In true PT style, the 'conductor' repeats the key points related to the 'narrator' (subtly correcting or clarifying any points that may have been related incorrectly or ambiguously) so that the 'actors' and the 'audience' have the benefit of hearing the information a second time. (This would be at least the third time they have been presented with this information, the first time being during class time.) The 'conductor' then asks the 'narrator' to choose which 'actor' will play each world leader.

- *Setting up*: The 'conductor' will have provided props that the 'actors' can use and at this time the 'actors' who have been assigned roles choose any objects that will aid them in personifying their character.
- *Enactment*: The 'conductor' uses the transitory phrase 'Let's watch!' and the 'actors' work together to portray her/his character's involvement in the events leading up to World War I. For those teachers who have concerns about the 'actors' forgetting events or facts, the PT framework has a built-in safety guard: if the scene begins to lose focus or begins to portray facts erroneously, the 'conductor' simply asks the 'actors' to pause and then asks the 'narrator' if there are parts of the enactment that need clarification, elaboration or change. This gives everyone time to get back on track and portray the facts faithfully.
- *Acknowledgement:* Once the bulk of the information has been acted out and if the 'actors' do not pause, the 'conductor' can step in to determine whether they have reached a natural stopping place, at which time the 'actors' will assume the gesture of acknowledgement towards the 'narrator'.
- *Returning to the narrator:* The 'conductor' will direct the 'narrator' to report on whether any inconsistencies have been noticed, giving everyone one more opportunity to repeat sections that need adjustments. The 'conductor' will then address the 'actors' and ask them to readdress those areas.
- *New interviews, enactments and acknowledgments:* The 'conductor' will choose a different 'narrator', different 'actors' (preferably others who need a review in the subject using physical intelligence), and will again ask for suggestions of another unit to focus on. The process then begins again.
- *Closing sequence, review, and a farewell:* At the end of the session, the 'conductor' can ask each group of 'actors' to return to the stage and repeat key points of the unit that they have brought to life. The 'conductor' can also use this opportunity to elaborate or clarify certain points of each unit covered.

## Maths

- *The Narrator*: A student who is strong in logical intelligence.
- *Actors*: Four or five students who have demonstrated difficulties in the subject.
- *Conductor*: The teacher.
- *Musician*: Same as in the first scenario.
- *Prologue*: Same as in the first scenario.
- *Presentation of Actors*: Same as in the first scenario.
- *Ice-breaking games with audience*: The teacher (now the conductor) might present some logic or critical thinking problems, keeping the tone light and helping the students break down whatever resistance they may have towards the subject.
- *Choosing the theme*: The teacher can let the students choose the mathematical function to be focused on. In this case, the focus is on geometric shapes.
- *Fluid Structure of Verbal Stimulus from Audience Members*: Same as in the first scenario.
- *First Interview*: The 'conductor' asks the 'narrator' to give the definition of various geometric shapes. The 'actors' pay close attention in order to be able to physically present each one. The 'conductor' repeats the definitions (subtly clarifying any that may have been related ambiguously), so that the 'actors' and the 'audience' have the benefit of hearing the information yet one more time. The 'conductor' then asks the 'narrator' to assign roles (shapes) to the 'actors'.
- *Setting up*: The 'conductor' will have provided props which the 'actors' can use and at this time those who have been assigned roles choose any objects that will aid them in manifesting the shapes.
- *Enactment*: When the 'conductor' feels that the scene is set, the transitory phrase 'Let's watch!' is spoken. In this case, the interaction between the 'actors' is a bit different. Each 'actor' has been assigned a geometric shape and so that person will direct the others in how to form it on the stage. Once one shape has been formed and the definition given, the next 'actor' takes charge and another geometric shape is presented. At any time

the 'conductor' can intercede if a shape or definition is forgotten or presented incorrectly, but in general, the actors work together, clarifying and adjusting each shape.

- *Acknowledgement:* Once all the shapes named and defined by the 'narrator' have been presented, the 'actors' face the 'narrator' and make the appropriate posture of acknowledgement.

- *Returning to the narrator:* The 'conductor' will then direct the 'narrator' to report on whether the shapes have been accurately formed and defined. If there are any inconsistencies, the 'narrator' will repeat the definition and the 'conductor' will ask the 'actors' to readdress those areas.

- *New interviews, enactments and acknowledgments:* The 'conductor' will then choose a different 'narrator', different 'actors', and will ask the 'audience' to decide on another unit, which will then be developed.

- *Closing sequence, and a farewell:* The 'conductor' asks each group of 'actors' to return to the stage and repeat the mathematical functions that they have brought to life.

## Conclusion

This chapter has expounded on the components and framework of a Playback Theatre session and how it can be used quite effectively by teachers who follow the CLIL methodology. Included are specific examples of the use of this theatrical format with adult audiences and high school students, both with the goal of creating community and with a stress on demonstrating the importance of PT in the practice of being able to express oneself and in being heard. Explanations of the suitability of PT in the educational format have been presented with concrete ways of applying the structure in a CLIL classroom. PT is an optimal application of the CLL methodology for the development and promotion of interactive, communicative and creative key skills.

# References

Barreto, G. 2008. *El teatro Playback: talleres de improvisación teatral para la integración de los inmigrantes latinoamericanos en Montreal*. Université de Montreal. Département de littératures et de langues modernes. Faculté des Arts et des Sciences.

Bett, R. 2000. Playback in Western Australian Prisons. *Interplay* X/3, 3.

Cox, D. 1996. I can see playback working. *Interplay* VI/1, 6.

Day, F. 1998. Rehabilitation: Disability. *Interplay* VIII/3, 4.

Dennis, R. 2004. *Public performance, personal story: a study of playback theatre*. Doctoral thesis. Brisbane: Griffith University, Faculty of Education.

Feldhendler, D. 2005. *Théâtre en miroirs, l'histoire de vie mise en scène*. Paris: Téraèdre.

_____. 2006. La vie mise en scène, théâtre et récit. *Le français dans le monde Sondernummer Recherches et applications* 39, 155–168.

_____. 2007. Playback Theatre. A Method for Intercultural Dialogue. *Scenario*, 2.

Friedler, R. 2006. Una pasión vislumbrada en Nepal: el Teatro Playback. Diálogo con Jonathan Fox. *Hojas de Psicodrama*, July, 5–10. <http://aepág.fidpág.net/sites/aepág.fidpág.net/files/hojas_de_psicodrama_54_jul_2006_0.pdf > Accessed 4 March 2014.

Fox, H. 2007. Playback Theatre: Inciting Dialogue and Building Community through Personal Story. *Drama Review*, 51/ 4T 196, 89–105.

Fox, J. 1994. *Acts of service: Spontaneity, commitment, tradition in the non-scripted Theatre*. New Paltz, NY: Tusitala.

_____. 1999. A Ritual for our Time. In Fox, Jonathan/ H. Dauber. *Essays on Playback Theatre*. New Platz, NY: Tusitala Publishing, 116–134.

_____ / Dauber, H. (eds). 1999. *Gathering voices: Essays on Playback Theatre*. New Platz, NY: Tusitala Publishing.

Hofman, H. 1997. Playback Theatre as an action method in training and education for organizations. *Playback in Organizational*

*Development*, Deventer, Holland. <http://www.playbackschool. org/rcsources longlist.htm> Accessed 5 June 2014.

Laferriére, G. / Motos, T. 2003. *Palabras para la acción.* Ciudad Real: Ñaque.

Larkinson, L. / Rowe, N. 2003. A 'playback theatre's project with users of mental health services. *A life in the day* 7/3.

Moran, G. / Alon, U. 2011. Playback theatre and recovery in mental health: Preliminary evidence. *The Arts in Psychotherapy* 38/5, 318–324.

Mehisto, P. / Marsh, D. / Frigols, M. 2014. *Uncovering CLIL: Content and Language Integrated Learning in Bilingual and Multilingual Education.* Oxford, England: Macmillan Education.

Motos, T. (ed). 2013. *Otros escenarios para el teatro.* Ciudad Real: Ñaque.

Muckley, L. 1998. Rehabilitation: Mental Health. *Interplay* VIII/3, 5.

Murphy, J. 2001. Playback Theatre in housing estates. *Interplay* XI/ (2), 9.

Oivo, M. *How Supervision can Support the Work of a Playback Theatre Leader.* Centre for Playback Theatre: building communities of understanding, <http://www.playbackcentre.org> Accessed 5 June 2014.

Park-Fuller, L. M. 2003. Audiencing the Audience: Playback Theatre, Performative Writing, and Social Activism, *Text and Performance Quarterly* 23/ 3, 288–310.

Robb, H. 2002. Conducting a refugee performance: A place to speak. *Interplay* XII/3, 11.

Rowe, N. 2007. *Playing the Other: Dramatizing Personal Narratives in Playback Theatre.* London: Jessica Kingley Publiser.

Salas, J. 2006. Doing Playback Theatre in a Foreign Language: Learning Language, Learning Culture, Learning Identity. *Playback Leadership.* New Paltz (NY): Centre for Playback Theatre.

Salas, J. 1993. *Improvising real life: Personal story in Playback Theatre.* New Platz, NY: Tusitala Publishing.

_____. 2005. Using Theater to Address Bullying. *Educational Leadership* 63/1, 78–82.

_____. 2008. *Do My Story, Sing My Song: Music therapy and Playback Theatre with troubled children*. New Platz, NY: Tusitala Publishing.

_____. 2009. Playback Theatre: A Frame for Healing. In David R. Johnson/ Renée Emunah, (eds). *Current Approach in Drama Therapy* (Second Edition). Springfield, Illinois: Charles C. Thomas Publisher Ltd, 445–459.

Southard, S. 2000. Climbing the Adobe Mountain. *Interplay* X/ 3, 8.

Stronks, D. 2014. *Teatro para el cambio en las organizaciones*. Ciudad Real: Ñaque. http://www.naque.es/virtuemart/178/16/ebook/man uales/teatro-para-el-cambio-en-las-organizaciones-detail.

Wright, P. 2002. *An investigation into Applied Theatre on Communities of Meaning with Specific Reference to Education and Health*. Thesis Ph D. University of New England.

Wynter, L. 1998. Rehabilitation: Youth. *Interplay* VIII/ 3, 6.

KEMAL SINAN ÖZMEN / CEM BALÇIKANLI

# Theatre Acting in Second Language Teacher Education

## Introduction

The idea of teaching foreign language teachers basics of acting and stage competence may trigger a thought-provoking question: Do we have enough time and energy to focus on yet another competence for teachers in second language teacher education (SLTE)? It is indeed quite reasonable to claim that SLTE programs have already been loaded with many different sorts of courses to cover and competences to imbue teachers. The incentive behind this chapter is to provide teacher trainers with ways of teaching theatre acting to student teachers in SLTE programs. Therefore, at the end of this chapter, we will together decide whether it is a burden or a must for a SLTE program to equip student teachers with basic skills of an actor.

Acting in teacher education is based on the viewpoint of 'teaching as a performing art', which is also the broadest name given to this field of inquiry. For at least four decades, teacher educators and trainers have discussed the similarities of acting and teaching (eg. Sarason, 1999). Most of these discussions have contributed to the literature in which the phenomenon was analysed and systematized in various ways. Educational researchers add to the literature, usually through research studies, action research, and personal narratives, as well as essays and books detailing the similarities and differences between the qualities that mark the highly effective teacher and the distinguished performing artist (Hart, 2007). Given the vast amount of variables involved in shaping student teachers' experiences, it is not surprising that most of the studies in 'teaching as a performing art' are qualitative (Eisner, 2002a, 2002b; Freidman, 1988; Griggs, 2001 Hart, 2007; Javidi, Downs &

Nussbaum, 1988; Sarason, 1999; Taylor, 1996; Van Tartwick, Brekel-
mans, & Wubbels, 1998).

Although the analogy of acting and teaching has never been a hot
area of research and practice in the last decades, taking teacher as a performance artist is not a currently suggested innovation for the literature
of teacher education. The art has played a role in general teacher education since John Dewey and the beginning of the progressive education
movement. For several decades, many educational researchers have acknowledged and examined the common grounds of performing artist
and the teacher (Dewey, 1934, Eisner, 1979; Freidman, 1988; Griggs,
2001; Hart, 2007; Sarason, 1999). However, the artistic aspect of teaching profession merits attention from teacher educators and trainers to
unravel dynamics of teaching profession related to performing arts, to
improve our understanding of creating and supporting the teacher identity in both pre and in-service teacher education, and to develop the
performance-related competences of teachers, such as effective use of
voice and body language and nonverbal awareness, just to name few.
Nevertheless, there is still a need for practical and doable tasks and
activities for trainers' classroom use.

The studies on teaching as a performing art may be grouped under three dimensions. The first and second dimensions were suggested
by Freidman (1988) in which he categorized the scholars who take the
teacher as an actor and classroom as theatre analogy as a *general dimension*. These studies generally focus on the artistic nature of teaching
profession by addressing metaphors and analogies. The second is the
*specific dimension* which refers to studies providing a detailed picture,
rigorously analysing these two professions in terms of both philosophy
and practice to reveal specific similarities and differences. We can add
a third dimension to categorize studies of acting and teaching professions, which we can call *instructional dimension*. Those are the studies
which actually borrow specific knowledge and skills from acting literature to equip teachers with critical competences such as use of voice
and body language, nature of improvisation and an animated communication or conscious coding of the nonverbal behaviour, and so forth. As
a matter of fact, teacher education lacks the insights of the instructional
dimension, and it is hardly possible for a teacher trainer to find a book to

learn about how to teach student teachers acting. For example decades ago, Lessinger and Gillis (1976) produced some materials to be utilized in teacher education for improving the acting skills of the teachers. Similarly but years later, Griggs (2003) suggested some acting activities which can be used in teacher training. Hart (2007) designed and applied a syllabus for the 'Teacher as a Performing Art' course. Finally, Ozmen (2010) prepared a complete acting course for English language teacher education programs with the syllabus, readings and all materials to be exploited by the trainer. In addition to providing the contemporary theoretical frame of 'teaching as a performing art' literature, this chapter also offers tasks and activities for teacher trainers to use in both pre-service and in-service courses.

## Teaching as a performing art

The literature of teaching as a performing art may first appear to be an extreme theoretical proposal or a fun but shallow area for practice. However, artistic aspects of teaching have been articulated by the outstanding figures of teacher education, who are widely recognized as influential *scientists*. To give examples, Barzun (1945) believed that teaching was artistic because effective teaching performance could produce aesthetic pleasure. Taylor (1954: 55) stated that teaching was an art to the extent that it was done imaginatively and stimulated "the young to explore the world of the imagination". James (1958: 23) asserted that "psychology is a science, and teaching is an art; and sciences never generate arts directly out of themselves". Taylor (1960) lamented that artistic aspect of education is neglected in both theory and practice. Similarly, Sanford (1967: 123) pointed out that the art of teaching had been ignored in education and "effective teaching is an art, one of the highest and most important arts we have". Taking the claim and discussion some steps further, Shamos (1970) mentioned that teaching was a mostly form of art. Other scholars of the field have discussed the teaching as an artistic profession by addressing aspects, such as its performance-based nature, improvisational aspects, its dynamic domains in terms of classroom interaction and aesthetic aspects in terms of verbal and nonverbal communication (Axelrod; 1973; Broudy, 1985; Dawe, 1984; Eble, 1977; Nisbet, 1977; Griggs, 2001; Hart, 2007; Özmen, 2011a).

Among all these supporters of idea of teaching as an artistic performance, Eisner (1979) made the strongest argument that teaching was purely an art. He underlined that teaching was artistic since the results of the teaching were often created in a process, and since it could be described as aesthetically when performed effectively: "It [teaching] is an art in the sense that teaching can be performed with such skill and grace that, for the student as well as for the teacher, the experience can be justifiably characterized by aesthetic" (Eisner, 1979: 151). According to Lowman (1984), classrooms are arenas where the teacher is the focal point, just as the actor or orator on a stage, teaching is undeniably a performing art. Similarly, Highet's (1958) remarks on the issue give us not only the heart of teaching profession, but also the vital aspects of teaching that are purely artistic: "I believe that teaching is an art, not a science [...] Teaching is not like inducing a chemical reaction; it is much more like painting a picture [...] You must throw your heart into it, you must realize that it cannot be all done by formulas, or you will spoil your work, and your pupils, and yourself" (1958: 8).

To articulate some well-grounded analogies, it was commonly accentuated that both teachers and performing artists realized their work by utilizing their selves and communicating with a group of people (Burns, 1999; Dennis, 1995; Hanning, 1984; Jarudi, 2000; Lessinger & Gillis, 1976; Rives Jr., 1979). Also effective teachers and artists were claimed to need to capture and hold the attention and interest of their audiences (DeLozier, 1979; Hanning, 1984). Both professionals also follow and perform a script, which is the play script for the actor and the lesson plan for the teacher (Rives Jr., 1979). Both teachers and actors perform their job on a setting as a primary performance area: mostly the stage for the actor and the classroom for the teacher (Rives Jr., 1979; Van Tartwick et al., 1998). Finally both professionals must achieve a communication which should result in an interactional process to fulfil the outcomes of the play script or the lesson plan (Burns, 1999; Rives Jr., 1979; Rose & Linney, 1992).

The theoretical discussions can be expanded but to offer a down-to-earth study of 'teaching as a performing art' literature, Hart (2007) reported on a study in which student teachers were taught some techniques and principles of acting. This was a promising attempt as Hart (2007) designed a course entitled 'Teaching as a Performing Art' and worked with some student teachers and teachers throughout the course. In addition to designing an acting course for student teachers, Hart (2007) found that theatre-based competences might be used to develop new teacher identities and to help student teachers overcome performance obstacles in teaching. Developing a strong teacher identity and overcoming problems and flaws in teacher communication will lead us to develop effective teaching strategies in the classroom. Various studies on entangling the nature of the effective teaching found that the dynamics of effective teaching resemble those of performing artists (Jarudi, 2000; Justen, 1984; Tauber, Mester, & Buckwald, 1993). It is essential that student teachers do the work of performing artist to be effective performers (Tauber & Mester, 2007).

Research by Javidi, Downs and Nussbaum (1988) on the utilization of the dramatic devices by award-winning teachers revealed that "A teacher who is dramatic within classroom leads his or her students in identifying relevant material presented during lectures" (Javidi et al., 1988: 279). The results indicated that:

- Award-winning teachers use dramatic behaviours (humour, self-disclosure and narrative) in a fifty-minute lecture, primarily in parallel with the content of the course;
- Non award-winning teachers use humour less frequently than award-winning teachers;
- Although award-winning teachers use self-disclosure and narrative more than non award-winning teachers, it must be underlined that the award-winning teachers on the high school and college levels utilized this sort of behaviour remarkably more than award-winning teachers on the mid-high school level (Javidi et al., 1988).

This research illustrates that acting techniques exploited to support the course content and purposes are among the elements of effective teaching. However, the question of how these award-winning teachers came to that level of teaching performance still needs a scholarly answer. Were they aware of the specific techniques they utilized? Were they dramatic outside the classroom? How many of these dramatic devices leading them to become effective teachers were the outcome of the teacher education they received? The current zeitgeist of the field at least informs us that a teacher with basic competences of an actor can operate following critical classroom behaviours that promote learning (Özmen, 2010):

•     Using body language and voice as an instructional tool;
•     Being able to observe learners' nonverbal communication flow effectively;
•     Coding nonverbal messages consciously to promote learning;
•     Establishing a consistent teacher identity to perform;
•     Securing the attention of their audiences;
•     Encouraging students (audience) to participate actively,
•     Trying to create an atmosphere which is necessary for the instruction of the course content.

There is no doubt that the task of the teachers is far heavier than that of the actors owing to the fact that actors face a specific audience once or twice. However, teachers are to perform their 'teacher self' with the same group of people sometimes for months, or even for years at undergraduate level of instruction. This is a persuasive indicator of the need for a strong and a consistent 'teacher identity', which will establish a ground for turning all the efforts spent for successful classroom performances to beneficial and meaningful ones. From a different point of view, teachers are not as lucky as actors in their training in that most of the input provided for the student teachers concerning their performance stay at a feedback level; that is to say, even if a reflective practice (Wallace, 1991) is adopted in a given SLTE program, student teachers are not educated about how to use their body language and voice effectively (Özmen, 2011b). If you are a teacher trainer, it is most likely that you have already read some suggestions in the teacher training books, such as 'use your voice and body language effectively' or 'look confident but not threatening', or 'establish a vivid, friendly atmosphere'. However, the problem is that if student teachers are not trained about how to use their voice and body language effectively, how are they going to do so? How can they possible reach awareness in nonverbal communication without any training about it? Here a solution to such problems may be found in the literature of teaching as a performing art.

In this respect, most of the teacher's work in the classroom is all about establishing the right atmosphere with full awareness of nonverbal communication flow and with effective utilization of teacher's voice and body language for an animated communication. To give an example of what we mean by classroom atmosphere, let's recall the famous experiment known as 'The Dr. Fox Effect'. An actor was introduced to a conference audience as Dr. Myron L. Fox, and he presented a very enthusiastic lecture which contained little or no content by using double-talk and by giving incongruous and irrelevant examples (Perry, 1985). This professional actor delivered three lectures to three separate audiences as Dr. Fox. The results revealed that the audiences highly rated the lecture, claiming that, besides other impressive aspects, the lecture stimulated their thinking (Tauber & Mester, 2007), and simply no one realized that it was a fake presentation (Clark, 2005). Even some of the audience claimed to have read Dr. Fox's previous studies. This experiment should be analyzed from two different aspects. First, the results clearly illustrate that an effective teaching performance can have a very strong effect on the attention, motivation and participation of the students. Remember that Dr. Fox is a professional actor trained to communicate a group of people by using his voice and body language skilfully and aesthetically. Moreover, he was also trained to observe the reactions of the audience and to shape his verbal and nonverbal messages accordingly. In addition to all these, he can *consistently* perform the role of a conference presenter. Second, whether a teacher, an actor, or a conference speaker, the acting skills of a performer are precious when used to make the content and purposes of the course accessible and learnable for the students. The thin line between 'fun for the sake of fun and 'fun for the sake of learning' should be established by the acting teacher very carefully. This can be done only when the consistent and autonomous teacher identity is set up by the teacher. Only then, can the attention of the students be secured and maintained for the course content.

## Acting methods in teacher education

The pursuit of designing acting activities for teacher education is generally based on the studies of Stanislavski, who constructed the contemporary methodology of acting (Griggs, 2001; Hart, 2007; Lessinger & Gillis, 1976; Travers, 1979). Apart from the works of Stanislavski, many other theoreticians of acting literature have been referred in the teacher education research. American theater director Anne Bogart and famous acting teacher Viola Spolin are some of the artists. In addition, another eminent figure is Eric Morris, an American actor and an acting coach, whose books on acting are widely used in teacher education (Özmen, 2011a).

Contributions of Stanislavski to contemporary theatre acting are invaluable on the grounds that he constructed a theory which has had a great impact on all actors and directors not only on stage but also on silver screen as well. His acting methodology is known as 'The Method' and still acknowledged as the major methodology of acting. We strongly believe that his acting methodology may contribute to teacher education in many ways. Essentially, what Stanislavski created as a theory was a sound way of 'creating an identity'. Although his studies were centred on theatre acting, it is for sure that teacher education can benefit from his principles and certain techniques (Travers, 1979).

Travers (1979: 16) noted that "Stanislavski had essentially a complete theory of how a personality can be created in the adult". The process of creating a personality was defined as "a part of our organic natures. It is based on the laws of nature" (Stanislavski, 1949:279). Stanislavski (1972) believed that the primary task of an actor was to understand the inner mechanics of the target role. The process of analysing and understanding the inner mechanics, or the psychological structure, leads the actor to construct an authentic version of the role. The choices on voice and body language codes come at a later stage at which the actor has established the emotional bonds with the target role. Therefore, Stanislavski's proposal was not to create a superficial imitation of the role to be performed, but the actualization of a possible authentic and believable version of the role by analysing and internalizing the emotional dynamics and nature of the target character. "Superficial displays of anguish would be unconvincing to others if they were not accompanied by corresponding inner feelings" (Travers, 1979: 16–17). In this sense, he does not offer pretending, but becoming and being. In order to reach this level and mastery of acting, Stanislavki developed some certain techniques such as 'action', 'as if' and 'emotional recall' (Stanislavski, 1972). Now let's scrutinize student teachers in a typical English language teacher education program: Are they aware of the similarities and differences between their personal and professional selves? How much do they practice and think about how to establish an emotionally healthy and consistent professional identity? How much do teacher education programs invest in classroom selves of the student teachers? It is ironic to share the following remark of Travers these days when defining teacher and teaching in terms of competences is popular:

> Much of the so-called competency-based teacher education involves attempts to copy the superficial features of a role. Programs that teach the teacher to walk around the classroom and to hand out verbal equivalents of M&M's represent attempts to copy superficial features of the role. Stanislavski long argued that superficial features of a role do not have to be learned, for they appear automatically once the deeper structures have been developed (1979: 17).

Özmen (2010) conducted a study on using Stanislavski's acting method in English language teacher education in an experimental design and revealed that an acting course designed for student teachers facilitated 1) the use of nonverbal communication, nonverbal immediate behaviour, 2) awareness and control in using voice and body language in micro teaching demonstrations and 3) the emergence of teacher identity. The further studies on the same acting course also revealed that learning about the basics of acting contributes to changing beliefs about language learning and teaching (Özmen, 2011b). In another study, Özmen (2011a) offered a model of teacher identity development for teacher trainers to sequence the acting tasks in a rational order in their courses. BEING Model (Özmen, 2011a) was investigated in a qualitative study in which 3 student teachers were followed throughout an acting course in English teacher education program via narrative, observation, interview and simulations. Based on the acting methodology of Stanislavski (1949), the BEING Model is an acronym of five-stage model for teacher identity development, through which student teachers approximate to their teacher identities by practicing teaching and acting tasks. The stages of identity development via practising acting are given in Table 1.

| STAGES OF BEING | ROLES OF THE TRAINER | EXPECTED ATTITUDES OF THE TRAINEES |
|---|---|---|
| BELIEVE | Giving feedback for emotional preparation | Identifying an identity which one wishes to become |
| EXPERIMENT | Monitoring and eliciting rehearsed identity | Creating own version of the role |
| INVENT | Shaping the identities by reflections and feedback | Analyzing oneself carefully to discover required qualities |
| NAVIGATE | Providing group discussions and feedback for problem solving | Rehearsals in a practical situation |
| GENERATE | Feedback for identity that is developed, and identifying personal dispositions. | Constructing a flexible, democratic teacher identity that is open to change and innovation. |

Table 3.1. Developmental stages of Being Model.

The first phase, BELIEVE, is a self-observation process during which student teachers discover their target professional identity and *believe* they can achieve it. It is important for student teachers to observe their resources and the requirements of their target teacher identity so as to identify a reasonable and realistic target. This phase is an emotional grounding period depicted as a critical one for the actors (Stanislavski, 1949). EXPERIMENT is the second phase, and as the name suggests, the student teachers practiced acting tasks, activities and improvisations that are designed for teacher education. The third phase, INVENT, is a transitional one during which student teachers are asked to synthesize their acting knowledge with teaching and discover their own way of speaking and behaving in the classroom. This phase is the technical one for Stanislavski (1949) in which actors invent a unique voice and codes for body language. Therefore, in the INVENT stage, student teachers are led to discover their body language and voice so that they can actualize their target teacher identity not only at an emotional state but also at a physical state. These three phases are based on a cyclical relationship until the student teachers NAVIGATE the problems they encounter and move to the GENERATE phase, in which they display the evidence of an emerging teacher identity. The *navigate* phase is not based on any acting method, but added on purpose to offer a process for the classroom so that student teachers can solve the problems they come across and overcome any challenges while developing a strong teacher identity. For instance, a student teacher may experience difficulties about using voice, or controlling her emotions under some tense conditions. In such cases, the NAVIGATE phase offers student teachers extra tasks to overcome these problems likely to occur during the rehearsals of teacher identity. As stated above, the GENERATE phase is the result of these four initial phases and the first evidence of emotional and performance-related materialization of the target teacher identity are established by the student teacher. GENERATE phase is not a monolithic or a stable phase, but more like a dynamic process constantly interacting and negotiating with the experiences of student teacher. The Figure 1 shows how those phases are interrelated and function with regard to student teachers' identity construction process (See Özmen, 2011a for more information).

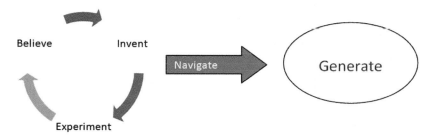

Figure 3.1. BEING Model in action.

One of the reasons why trainers do not use acting tasks in their teacher training courses is that it requires training on how to exploit such tasks and how to order them reasonably so as to yield an effective result in student teachers' development concerning both affective and performance-related issues. In this respect, the major objective of BEING Model is to help teacher trainers without any acting background to sequence the acting materials in their training courses and to offer the right material at the right time.

## Practical acting tasks for training courses

The following 10 acting tasks and 5 rehearsals have been exploited for more than five years in drama courses given by the teacher trainers at Gazi University, English Language Teaching program in Turkey. These tasks are designed to provide pre-service teacher trainees with a 14-week and 4-hour course on acting. Developing main acting skills enables student teachers to use their body language and voice more effectively and to construct their professional identities in a context in which this identity is analysed and rehearsed as a role. The major pedagogical objectives of the tasks are: effective communication skills (body language, use of voice and nonverbal communication), sensory awareness which is necessary for managing nonverbal communication and performing the target professional identity, emotional preparation necessary for realizing an effective teacher identity, nonverbal immediacy and finally a rehearsal process of teacher identity by blending these above-mentioned all. These objectives will be fulfilled by practising some actor-preparation activities, learning some major acting techniques and some various rehearsals on the teacher that student teachers are aspired to become. The following 10 tasks are given in detail along with their objectives and procedures. One should note that none of these tasks require any unusual materials, and what is more, most of them do not require any materials or accessories at all. Following these ten tasks, five tasks are called *Rehearsals* and described for the trainers as outside-the-class work for the individual student teacher's rehearsals for establishing a teacher identity.

### Task 1: Masks Off

The aim of the activity, as a warm-up, is to create an atmosphere in the class in which the student teachers may take risk and get rid of the usual atmosphere of a typical classroom. Also, this activity is used to increase the emotional sensitivity and empathy of the student teachers. Three chairs or any kind of three seats are required for the task.

Three chairs are placed in front of the class. Each chair represents an emotion: fear, anger and laughter respectively. A student teacher stands behind each chair, and her/his aim is to help those who will sit and try to act out the character of the chair. After the chairs and responsible trainees are ready, the class lines up and each trainee sits each chair at least one, as quickly as possible, so as to experience a sharp transition between emotions. Chair responsible whispers in their ears about possible occasions which may help the sitting student teacher catch the right feeling. The activity may continue until the trainer decides that the trainees break their usual trainee role.

### *Task 2: Light in the Blindness*

The aim of the activity is to raise awareness on the other people's existence and energy so that the requirement of 'cooperation' and 'feeling of us' may be created, and is used to help actors trust each other. This is also a cooler activity. Soft music may be useful for the necessary atmosphere.

The student teachers should be told that there are many things around which they can see only by closing their eyes, walk around slowly and by trying to focus. They are told to mingle in the classroom slowly, listen to the peers' footsteps, and their breathing and to pay attention to the existence of others. The more they get concentrated, the less small crashes they will face. At the end of the activity, the teacher asks about the experience: Whether they feel safe at first or not, or whether they feel different emotions.

Some space is needed for the student teachers to mingle in the classroom. The trainer uses soft music. No talking and interaction is allowed. The student teachers close their eyes and mingle in the classroom. They sometimes bump into each other, naturally laugh and talk. However, after a while, if a concentration reached, the participants will begin to feel people around them and even identify their friends. The trainer should be cautious about a possible accident because trainees will be mingling in the classroom without seeing their environment. Encouraging slow movement and monitoring them will be helpful for both aims of the activity and safety.

*Task 3: A Slow Motion Life*

The aim of the activity is to raise awareness on the observation skills of the student teachers on both themselves and others. The student teachers are also given the opportunity to practise body language and use voice skills. Preferably, the trainer divides the class into group of four or five, and assigns the same story, which the trainees will act out. This can be a very easy story, or improvisation, like you find yourself in a fight in a bus. During the activity, the improvisation will switch to a slow motion one with the signal of the trainer. There may be some certain levels of slow motion, like LEVEL 1 which is slow, LEVEL 2 very slow, and LEVEL 3 which is the slowest one. Assigning the same task to all groups may help the learners focus on the body language, and nonverbal communication, not the story and the anxiety of the creating a drama, say, in three minutes.

The trainer groups the class the way she wishes. The same improvisation theme is given to all groups and the activity is described to them. A signal for level transition is identified, like a bell or so on. Five minutes for preparation is given to each group for discussion and preparation. The trainer may act out level 1, 2 and 3 when giving instructions. The first and second group should be given detailed feedback for the body language used in slow motion phases of the activity so that the remainder groups may develop an insight and perform more effective activities.

*Task 4: Silence of Mirrors*

The aim of the activity is to observe and reflect the body language of others. This is also a powerful 'trust' activity. Pairs of trainees stand in the class and imitate each other in detail. One of the trainees imitates, and the other is the mirror. The mirror has to be as accurate as possible. The task of the imitated trainee is to exceed the limits of the mirrors by using an unusual body language. As a second step, the trainer assigns some emotions to imitated trainee, but basic and doable ones. Silence is very important to lead trainees to observe each other's body language.

The trainer pairs the classroom. She identifies the mirrors and imitators. The trainer states the rules of the activity: the mirror need to behave exactly like the imitator. She also mentions that it is very important for the mirrors to observe the body language of the imitators and reflect them as accurate as possible. After a 5 minute of exercise, pairs change their roles. At the end of the activity, the trainees discuss the activity and reflect upon what they felt. For making an effective use of this activity, the trainees should be informed that this activity is not a fun activity like a break-state game. The imitator and imitated should move in a harmony so that observation and bodily reflection skills may be practiced.

### Task 5: Work Your Fingers

The aim of the activity is to observe the body language of others and synchronize the movements with a peer. The need for guessing the following movement of a partner may lead to a development in one's observation skills. Pairs of trainees stand in the class. Just by touching each other's fingers, one leads the other in the classroom as she wishes. The other trainee has to keep following her and never lose the finger contact. When the trainer observes that the pairs can synchronize with each other, she may use music to lead the pairs and make the process more complicated. Also, trainer may use some certain signals to make pairs move faster or more slowly.

The trainees work in pairs. In the teaching space, pairs touch each other's finger tips. They are told that they never lose the fingertip contact. One trainee is the leading partner, who can independently move. The other partner has to follow his movements without losing the finger contact. The trainees should be explicitly told that the aim of the activity is guess the following behaviour of the leading student.

### Task 6: Happening

Happening activities are heart of actor preparation courses. In happening activities, actors create a scene, a frozen photograph, which tells a story.

The story can be very complicated or a simple one. Mostly, this depends on the creativity and ability of the actors. If the trainees are taught what a happening is and its endless possibilities, they may be more creative and successful. Happenings should be used as much as possible. The aim is to be a part of a whole as an actor; both observe yourself and others by carrying an emotional burden by acting. At the same time trainees become conscious of the place of their part in the whole, which generally enables actors to raise awareness on personal resources.

Groups work for creating a story of their 'photograph'. The story of the happenings may be given to the groups by the trainer so as to save time. However, if the story is created by the groups it is much better for some hundred reasons. Then they use teaching space to show their happening. The rest of the classroom works in pairs to decode the message in the happening and figure out the role and story of each character.

The trainer asks the groups to prepare a photograph from a story, a film or etc. They are supposed to prepare in such a way that the audience should observe different characters, flow of the story, and other details like before and after this moment. The groups are given five minutes to get prepared. Then they come in front of the class and compose their photograph by freezing. The rest of the classroom may walk in the picture, try to understand the situation and feel the atmosphere the happening group has created.

*Task 7: Walking in the Dwarf Village*

The aim of this activity is to develop the skills of observation, cooperation with the others, creative thinking. Creating an imaginative setting and sticking to it while moving may develop observation skills. The teaching space is a dwarf village, but these dwarfs are not taller than a finger. A trainee begins walking in the dwarf village, very carefully and silent since it is night and they are sleeping. Aim of the trainee is to walk across the village, from one back of the class to the board. Trainer signals when the trainee is about to step on a house. When the trainee reaches the board, another trainee begins crossing the village, but remembering the exact place of the imaginary house. As the trainees reach the board, the number of imaginary houses increases and the crossing task becomes complicated and hard.

The trainer explains to the class that they have to walk over a dwarf village. Every trainee has to add a new detail to the village by his movements. This detail can be a bridge, a small carriage in front of a house and so on. As the details increase, it gets difficult to walk through the dwarf village. The key point is to observe each and every trainee carefully not to make a mistake.

*Task 8: Home Sweet Home*

The aim of this activity is to develop the skills of observation, cooperation with the others, creative thinking. The teaching space is a house. The trainer enters the imaginary house and creates some parts of the house and exists. No talking is allowed. Then, one by one, each student teacher enters home and creates yet another part and possible probes in the house. However, they must be very careful with the previous imaginary parts and probes. The activity can be more challenging and fun if conducted as a competition. The trainees are told that they need to create an imaginary house. Each student teacher enters the imaginary house and creates at least one new detail in the house. As the number of trainees increase, the details of the imaginary house become complicated to follow and remember. If a trainee forgets or violates any component of the house, s/he is dismissed. Each trainee should be given no more than 30 seconds in the house so that the class may walk into the house more than once. Also time limitation will make the activity more challenging.

*Task 9: Say What You Mean*

The aims of this activity are to be able to observe personal body language, and practice acting skills. As for the observing students, it is also an acquisition to watch what others perform in their parts. A small bell is needed for the task

Student teachers perform a language teaching activity in the classroom. This activity can be any of the activity that trainees have used in their previous micro and macro teaching attempts. In other words, they do not need to prepare an original teaching demonstration. When they hear the bell ringing they try to be inconsistent in terms of verbal and nonverbal communication they convey when teaching or simply talking with the classroom. When the teacher rings the bell again, they try to be consistent in their communication in terms of nonverbal and verbal messages.

The trainer describes the activity. S/he can demonstrate the activity to the students to make it clear for them as it is not a usual activity they have performed up to now. Then each student performs their teaching for 3 or 4 minutes at most. At the end of the activity, the experiences of the performing trainees are discussed in the classroom. The trainees are also warned not to exaggerate their performance. Their only aim is to perform consistency and inconstancy in their nonverbal communication deliberately and consciously.

*Task 10: Talk to Your Other Self*

Trainees come in front of the classroom and make us hear their inner self, how they feel, what they think and so on. Also the trainees can talk about how they look in terms of the nonverbal messages they convey. The trainer asks a trainee to perform one of her/his previous teaching demonstration, but this time the trainee will also talk about how she feels when she performs the activity. Trainee may talk about her feelings, her observations and any other relevant issues. This can be done by immediate shifts between usual utterances of the teaching demonstration and reflections of the trainee.

Surely some of the trainees will make fun of this activity. However, as the activity keeps performed in the classroom, it is likely that trainees will empathize with each other and pay more attention to the activity. That is why trainer should be patient. Also this activity may not be a suitable for some of the teacher trainees who display lack of self-confidence and esteem. Therefore, it may be wise to encourage those who are willing to perform the activity.

## Rehearsal 1: A writing task for teacher identity

This is an emotional preparation task, offering student teachers a metacognitive and an affective observation and questioning process. Student teachers are asked to write a reflective paper by answering these questions:

1. What are the similarities between your professional and personal selves?
2. What are the differences?
3. Which aspects of your teacher identity are admirable?
4. Which aspects of your teacher identity need some practice to make it better?
5. What kind of practices do you need to shape your teacher identity more effectively?
6. What strengths do you have to perform your teacher identity more effectively?
7. In what ways does your teacher self-communicate and interact with the students more skilfully?
8. In what ways does your teacher self-resolve conflicts and solve unexpected situations in the classroom?
9. How would your students define you?
10. How would your colleagues define you?

## Rehearsal 2: Observing Personal and Professional Selves

This task is designed to lead student teachers to observe the target identity (their teacher identity in the future) and analyze it in terms of the personal resources, desires and motivations. Student teachers work individually on the chart provided below. They should be informed that they will be thinking about their professional identity as a role to be performed. Before the writing task, student teachers are to write short responses to the table, then they are invited to write a paper based on the leading questions provided below:

|    | Characteristic | Personal Identity | Professional Identity |
|----|----------------|-------------------|-----------------------|
| 1  | Similarities | | |
| 2  | Differences | | |
| 3  | Admirable aspects | | |
| 4  | Strengths | | |
| 5  | Some aspects needing practice | | |
| 6  | Communication and interaction skills | | |
| 7  | Strategies for problem solving | | |
| 8  | Define yourself | | |
| 9  | Your students' definition of you | | |
| 10 | Your colleagues' definition of you | | |

Table 3.2. An analysis of personal and professional identities.

1. What are the similarities between your professional and personal selves?
2. What are the differences?
3. Which aspects of your teacher identity are admirable?
4. Which aspects of your teacher identity need some practice to make it better?
5. What kind of practices do you need to shape your teacher identity more effectively?
6. What strengths do you have to perform your teacher identity more effectively?
7. In what ways does your teacher self-communicate and interact with the students more skilfully?
8. In what ways does your teacher self-resolve conflicts and solve unexpected situations in the classroom?
9. How would your students define you?
10. How would your colleagues define you?

*Rehearsal 3: Identifying Personal Sources and Motivations*

This task is designed to lead student teachers to identify the personal sources, strengths and motivations so as to construct their teacher identity to be performed in their professional lives. Student teachers are invited to work individually on the questions below and prepare a paper. They will be reflection on what aspects of their personal identity will be the infrastructure and pillars for their professional identity. Then the papers will be separated to pairs of students and will be discussed in the classroom. The leading questions are as follows:

1.  What are your personal resources to be used for the effective construction of the teacher identity or the role that you will perform?
1.1.  Physical resources: body language, voice, appearance, unique gestures and postures you have invented, or any other accessories teaching materials that will assist you to perform your role.
1.2.  Emotional resources: What is your source of motivation for constructing your ideal teacher identity and act it out? Think about your reasons.
1.3.  Intellectual resources: What intellectual resources do you have apart from your field knowledge? Think about the books, poems or anything relevant that have an impact on constructing your teacher identity.
1.4.  Outer resources: What opportunities can you take in your department, or in your school in the future that may contribute to your teacher identity? Think about your education on teaching, professional development opportunities in the future and so on.

*Rehearsal 4: Identifying the Teacher Role*

This task is designed to lead student teachers to decide on their teacher identity by referring to their work on the previous three rehearsal activities. They are asked to describe their attitudes, reactions and general mood in the various teaching context in terms of the 15 variables. Those variables are based on observable teacher behaviours in the classroom, and student teachers are expected to provide their DOs and DONTs in such cases in the classroom. The task can be conducted in the classroom as a brainstorming activity, and then student teachers can write a response paper to describe their attitudes in each case.

1.  Conducting an activity
2.  Responding to students' questions
3.  Listening to students.
4.  Warning students about an important case
5.  Lecturing
6.  Monitoring
7.  Talking pairs and groups
8.  Talking individuals
9.  Reacting to an unexpected and unusual situation
10. Talking privately after the class
11. Giving feedback about assignments
12. Using voice
13. Using gestures and mimics
14. Managing nonverbal communication

*Rehearsal 5: Rehearsing the Teacher Identity*

This task is based on performing various rehearsals on the teacher identity, the target role student teachers have decided best and most suitable for them. After completion of the previous four rehearsal activities, student teachers will do some experiments on the teacher identity they have identified in the demonstrations and teaching attempts they have performed.

The student teachers may have their various teaching demonstrations video recorded to be utilized as a source in the acting class. If a video is provided by a student teacher, that will be an invaluable resource for the trainer and class to discuss the differences between what the trainee performed and what s/he aimed to perform. Therefore, trainer may ask to bring in their video recordings to the acting course. Apart from giving feedback to previous rehearsals on video, trainer assigns some small scale teaching attempts in which the focus will be on the performance of the trainee. Also trainers will assign pairs a drama teaching practice. Please see the lesson plan provided below. All the phases of this macro teaching practice will be prepared by the pairs of trainers, and this demonstration will be the actual and final performance of their teacher role/identity. The criteria for the drama teaching practice are as follows:

1. Both trainees will act out their teacher identity; thus, they will wear and look accordingly.
2. Both trainees have to perform a different character in their drama activities such as a king or a princess and so on.
3. All parts (Pre, While and Post) of the lesson plan will be designed as a drama activity.
4. No unrealistic or extreme materials will be used.
5. During the micro teaching, the peers will act out the age group and they will behave as natural as possible.
6. Student teachers bear in mind that this teaching attempt is realized for the performance of the teacher roles/identities. Therefore, pedagogical content is of secondary importance.
7. The micro teaching will be video recorded and as a follow-up task, the class will watch it and discuss.

Preferably student teachers prepare demonstrations in a long period of time and report in about their studies to the trainer regularly. Giving adequate time for this final task is important in that they will be doing a lot of rehearsals as well as thinking about their teacher identity, which is a complete awareness process. Also this assignment will be the major production of the trainees; therefore, it merits more attention. After the completion of the drama demonstrations, the student teachers watch the demos once again on video and discuss.

## A Sample of Integrated Drama Lesson Plan

*DRAMA ACTIVITY: After the murder of Mr. Whiskas Catmund*

<u>Level:</u> Pre – Intermediate to Advanced
<u>Age :</u> Adolescent/Adult
<u>Skills:</u> Integrated Skills

*Materials:* Some accessories for actors and actresses, Pictures of a cat, (1) National Anthem, (2) Oath in the court, (3) Top secret letters, (4) Life saver notes

*Story:*

Democratic Dictator General Atkinson's dearest cat Mr. Whiskas Catmund was murdered. While General was having milk bath with his brave soldiers between 09:00 and 10:00 in the morning, those who intended to hurt General ate Mr. Whiskas Catmund. However, "No crime shall be tolerated!" said General. Having identified some miserable suspects, he immediately established an independent military court and devoted his precious time to uncover the masks of evil criminals. Only then, perhaps, Mr. Whiskas could rest in peace.

*Procedure:*

Military court has started questioning the suspects immediately after the murder. Now, suspects are in front of the jury, trying to answer the questions of General and the jurors.

*Steps:*
The teacher will act out General Atkinson so that s/he can conduct the drama activity effectively. The role cards will lead students to know their part and act accordingly in the activity. Before the drama activity, the students are introduced to the story of the activity, and also they will be briefly introduced to the utterances to be utilized by the suspects.

1.  Character & Story intro: General Atkinson enters. Trial begins with the National Anthem* (See Materials) National Anthem is repeated (at least 3 times) until General Atkinson is satisfied.
2.  General summarizes the situation and gives top-secret letters*(Role cards. See materials) to the citizens who has a duty in the trial.
3.  Welcoming suspects to the front.
4.  Suspects vows (Vows are repeated by the class also, at least 3 times) with the help of the jurors and General.
5.  Trial Begins. General, advocators and jurors ask questions.
6.  Finding the murderer.

*Language & Skills involved:*

- Certain utterances are used in the drama activity in a controlled sense, mainly by focusing on pronunciation and speaking skills.
- Production /Free speaking activity mainly aiming at revising "Past Progressive Tense"
- Can be used as PRE or POST of a lesson plan.
- The level of the activity can be adapted at any language learning level.
- The aim of this revision activity can be adjusted by the teacher: any kind of Past tense, Past modals can be revised.

*MATERIALS (Role cards, Flash cards, some probes)*

*1. National Anthem*

I don't like to know
I don't like to hear
I don't like to see
This the way we're happy

General Atkinson is the key
He can make us free
Living in this country
is our lovely destiny!

*2. Oath in the Court*

Here to 1 swear my service to General
In peace or war
In living or dying
I'll be living with this code
Until our General releases me
Or death takes me

*3. Top-secret letters*

*3.1 Letters for Jurors*

You are chosen as a jury member. No! Do not cry until you finish your holly task. Your duty is to observe the suspects carefully and guess the murderer. Do not forget! Somebody has eaten Mr. Whiskas Catmund.

*3.2*

You're a suspect! Somebody saw you playing with Mr. Whiskas Catmund between 09:00 and 11:00. You used to have a cat but it deserted you, so you hate cats.

*3.3*

You are a suspect. Somebody saw you playing with Mr. Whiskas Catmund between 09:00 and 11:00.You love cats so much, but you are allergic to them. Between 09:00 and 11:00, you were having brunch with your friends.

*3.3*

You are the murderer. You were enjoying your barbecue. Suddenly, Mr.Whiskas Catmund fell over it from a tree. Its death was just an accident. You can ask for mercy from General Atkinson.


# Conclusions

It is time to answer the question posed at the beginning of this chapter: Is it a burden or a must to teach basics of acting to foreign language teachers? However, just like an artist would do, we will not offer you a deductive answer, perhaps rhetorically portraying the literature of 'teaching as a performing art' as an indispensable part of second language teacher education. Rather, it would be wiser to discuss why foreign language teachers need to learn some acting techniques in terms of what is generally missing in their pre-service and in-service education and what they really need in front of their learners. To this end, a perspective based on what researchers offer and what practitioner trainers say about this issue will help us make right choices of content and methodology for teaching acting to student teachers as well as teachers on the job.

In determining the value of borrowing certain techniques and philosophy of acting for teacher education, two major aspects of teaching a foreign language and teacher education seem critically important. One aspect is the need for providing student-teachers in STLE programs with a context of learning in which they can ponder over who they are, what recourses they have and who they want to become as a teacher. The following step of such an atmosphere of teacher education is to find opportunities to rehearse the target teacher identity under supervision and mediation. This brings us to the idea of developing teacher identities in pre-service education (Özmen, 2010). Eschewing from the acrimony of academic debate and fallacy of generalization, it is our observation that novice teachers encounter many problems in their classrooms due to lack of an established teacher identity, the development of which is mostly left to the mercy of socialization process in the given institution and experiences without reflection and feedback in a broader sense. The other aspect is the technical dimensions of the teacher communication in the classroom, which are the use of body language and voice, awareness of nonverbal communication and competences required to manipulate nonverbal codes used in instruction and observation skills including self-observation. Those technical aspects of teacher communication are well known to be influential in learners' motivation, affective learning and cognitive learning (Özmen, 2010).

In this respect, the tasks and rehearsals offered in this chapter aim at both of these aspects, both affective development process of teacher identity and acting practices that help develop a control over body language, voice and nonverbal communication. Although it may be quite confusing for a teacher trainer to bring in some acting tasks in their training classrooms, those tasks provided in this chapter are well-ordered in a way to lead student-teachers as well as teachers on the job throughout the basics of acting. In addition, the rehearsals are designed to create an experiential learning process, including affective and cognitive development processes of an emerging teacher identity. We are quite sure that teacher trainers can use those tasks and rehearsals to expand the repertoire of their teaching menu. Therefore, trainers who cannot offer a complete course on this issue can easily use those tasks individually in their regular courses.

The content and context of SLTE programs all around the world vary dramatically and accordingly the need for an instruction on acting cannot be similar for each of those contexts. However, the extent to which a given SLTE program feels a need to develop teacher identity or an animated communication for its graduates depends on certain questions: 'Can our SLTE program offer a set of courses in which our student-teachers think about and practice their professional identities?', 'Except from advises and feedback, do we really practise body language and voice for instructional purposes in our methodology course?', 'Do our student teachers really know how to use their dramatic devices to teach English?' Answers to these and similar questions will determine whether and to what extent a STLE program should teach acting in their courses.

# References

Axelrod, J. 1973. *The University Teacher as Artist*. San Francisco: Jossey Bass.

Barzun, J. 1945. *Teacher in America*. New York: Doubleday.

Broudy, H. S. 1985. In Box. *Chronicle of Higher Education 27*.

Burns, M. U. 1999. *Notes on How an Actor Prepares*. < http://www.nea.org/he/advo99/advo9910/feature.html> Accessed 18 January 2013.

Clark, R. W. 2005. The physics teacher: Sliders, staircases, and seduction. *Journal of Chemical Education 82/2*, 200.

Dawe, H. A. 1984. Teaching: A performing Art. *Phi Delta Kappan 65*, 548–552.

Dennis, A. 1995. *The Articulate Body: The Physical Training of the Actor*. New York: Drama Book.

DeLozier, M. W. 1979. The Teacher as Performer: The Art of Selling Students on Learning. *Contemporary Education 51/ 1*, 19–25.

Dewey, J. 1934. *Art as Experience*. New York: Minton, Balch & Co.

Eble, K. 1977. *The Craft of Teaching*. San Francisco: Jossey-Bass.

Eisner, E. 1979. *The Educational Imagination*. New York: Macmillan.
____. 2002a. *The Arts and the Creation of the Mind*. New Haven, CT: Yale University Press.
____. 2002b. What Can Education Learn from the Arts About the Practice of Education?. *Journal of Curriculum and Supervision* 18/ 1, 4–16.
Freidman, A. C. 1988. *Characteristics of effective theatre acting performance as incorporated into effective teaching performance*. Unpublished Doctoral Dissertation. Saint Louis University, Missouri.
Griggs, T. 2001. Teaching as Acting: Considering Acting as Epistemology and Its Use Teaching and Teacher Preparation. *Teacher Education Quarterly* 28/ 2, 23–37.
Hanning, R. W. 1984. *The Classroom as the Theatre of Self: Some Observations for Beginning Teachers* <www.ade.org/ade/bulletin/N077/077033.htm>. Accessed 07 December 2013.
Hart, R. 2007. Act like a teacher: Teaching as a Performing Art. *Electronic Doctoral Dissertations for UMass Amherst*.
Highet, G. 1958. *Art of Teaching*. New York: Vintage.
James, W. 1958. *Talk to Teachers*. New York: W. W. Norton.
Jarudi, L. 2000. *Academics Learn Dramatics From A.R.T.'s Houfek*. <http://www.hno.harvard.edu/gazette1999/03.25/teaching.html>. Accessed 17 December 2013.
Javidi, M. / M., Downs, V. C. / Nussbaum, J. F. 1988. A Comparative Analysis of Teachers' Use of Dramatic Style Behaviours at Higher and Secondary Educational Levels. *Communication Education* 37/4, 278–288.
Lessinger, L. M. / Gillis, D. 1976. *Teaching as a Performing Art*. Dallas, TX: Crescendo Publications.
Lowman, J. 1984. *Mastering the Techniques of Teaching*. San Francisco: Jossey-Bass.
Nisbet, L. 1977. The Ethics of the Art of Teaching. In S. Hook (ed). *The Ethics of Teaching and Scientific Research*. Buffalo: Prometheus, 125–127.
Özmen, K. S. 2010. Fostering nonverbal immediacy and teacher identity of English teacher trainees. *Australian Journal of Teacher Education* 36, 1–23.

_____. 2011a. Acting and teacher education: BEING model for identity development. *Turkish Online Journal of Qualitative Inquiry* 2/ 2, 36–49.

_____. 2011b. The impact of an acting course on prospective teachers' beliefs about language teaching. *Eurasian Journal of Educational Research* 45, 89–106.

Perry, R. P. 1985. Instructor expressiveness: Implications for improving teaching. In J. G. Donald/ A. M. Sullivan (eds). *Using research to improve teaching.* San Francisco: Jossey-Bass, 35–49.

Rose, K. / Linney, M. 1992. Teaching & Acting: the Performance of Understanding. *Liberal Education* 78/3, 24–27.

Sanford, N. 1967. *Where Colleges Fail.* San Francisco: Jossey-Bass.

Sarason, S. B. 1999. *Teaching as Performing Art.* New York: Teachers College Press.

Shamos, M. H. 1970. The Art of Teaching Science. In W. Morris (ed). *Effective College Teaching.* Washington: American Council on Education, 82–83.

Stanislavski, C. / Hapgood, E. R. 1949. *Building a Character.* New York: Theatre Arts Books.

_____. 1972. *An Actor Prepares.* New York: New York. Theatre Arts Books. (Original work published 1922).

Tauber, R. T. / Mester, C. S. / Buckwald, S. C. 1993. The Teacher as Actor: Entertaining to Educate. *NASSP Bulletin* 77/ 551, 20–28.

Tauber, R. T. / Mester, C. S. 2007. *Acting Lessons for Teachers: Using Performance Skills in the Classroom.* 2$^{nd}$ edition. Westport, Conn: Praeger.

Taylor, H. 1954. *On Education and Freedom.* Carbondale: Southern Illinois University Press.

_____. 1960. *Art and the Intellect.* New York: Teachers College Press.

Taylor, P. 1996. Rebellion, Reflective Turning and Arts Education Research. In P. Taylor (ed). *Researching Drama and Arts Education: Paradigms and Possibilities.* Washington, D.C.: Falmer Press, 1–21.

Travers, R. M. W. 1979. Training the Teacher as a Performing Artist. *Contemporary Education* 51/ 1, 14–18.

Wallace, M. 1991. *Training Foreign Language Teachers: A Reflective Approach.* Cambridge: Cambridge University Press.

Patricia Martín Ortiz

# Developing creativity through the *Mantle of the Expert* technique: A personal experience

## Introduction

> The young child who is totally open-minded, who adores drawing and painting and who colors all things, who asks incessant questions, and who can imagine that the bow in which his birthday present came is an infinite variety of things, including an airplane, a house, a cave, a tank, a boat, a spaceship gradually becomes trained to write notes in only one color, to ask very few questions (especially not "stupid" ones- that is, the most interesting ones!), to keep the millions of lusting-for-action muscle fibers still for hours on end, and to become increasingly aware of his incompetences in art, singing, intelligence and physical sports. In time the child thus graduates into an adult who considers himself uncreative, and who has 'progressed' from being able to think of millions of uses for a bow to being able to think of hardly any uses for anything (Buzan 2001: 39).

In the context of teaching a course for student teachers taking a degree in English, one of the main objectives I look for is to develop their creativity, to encourage them to be as imaginative as they were in their childhood and not just follow the points mentioned in the curriculum. The purpose of this chapter is to present one of the workshops which I carried out devoted to CLIL, specifically in Arts and Crafts, where I decided to use *The Mantle of the Expert* technique created by Dorothy Heathcote which was an experience which went beyond language.

In the first part I will deal with the concept of creativity; emphasizing its importance in all fields of life and not only in the school environment, showing the vision of several authors and also the different ways of stimulating learning in a creative way, revising the *Multiple Intelligences* theory by Gardner and also considering the prevalence of one or the other brain hemisphere and their link with the different skills according to Sperry and Ornstein. I will show drama as a fundamental technique in the field of teaching, making reference to some writers who focus on this topic and we will also remember the birth of drama companies in the Anglo-Saxon educative context from the thirties. Secondly, we will revise the use of drama in the teaching of foreign languages, analysing the work of Alan Maley and his novel proposal of activities which stimulate students' creativity. Finally, we will focus on the innovative and outstanding figure in the education field that is Dorothy Heathcote and her *Mantle of the Expert* technique. In the second part I will describe a practical experience carried out with students where we got involved in the preparations of an unexpected wedding which took place in Struay, a fictitious island of Scotland.

## Theoretical basis

### What is creativity?

> Creativity to me means mess, freedom, jumbled thoughts, words and deeds each fighting to claim their own space in my mind, and deciding, given even small amounts of free time, whether I shall write, paint, draw, take off to the beach with a camera, run outside, turn my house upside down to create a new environment, plant a garden or plan a new business. Or in a more formal sense it is the original thought, the spark, the ignition, the original design concepts or the blueprint (Thorne 2007: 17).

Creativity is basic in all the processes of human beings. Everybody is creative during childhood. We have our invisible friends, we can imagine dozen of uses for a cardboard box and the thousand forms a cloud in the sky may adopt. But then we are made, time and again, to colour the roof of the houses red and the sun yellow, to study the dates of battles instead of making a paper sword and fighting against our classmate sitting behind us living the battle, to quickly sum two plus three apples without giving us time to imagine the market stall where they are displayed: the yellow Golden Delicious apples, the redder Granny Smith, the wrinkled Bramley apples or the small Coxes. And later, when we read *Hamlet* and, instead of imagining ourselves in his place, feeling his doubt, crying for Polonius's death or saying our favourite sentence: 'There are more things in heaven and earth, Horatio, that are dreamt of in your philosophy', we have to write a commentary according to the model of the textbook, answer the questions as we are expected to do, without expressing our opinion and our feeling towards the play. Or we have to count the nouns or adjectives which appear in the text. Then many start to weaken and follow the adult world, so boring and offering so little place for fantasy and imagination.

## Developing creativity

In the last decades, there has been an increasing interest from authors to promote creativity in children. Kaye Thorne in her book *Essential creativity in the classroom* (2001) presents us with a passionate view about the issue of creativity in our lives. She focuses specially on the school environment, how we can help children to express their creativity, how to create a world of learning which is inspiring and motivating, and what teachers can do to stimulate creativity in the classroom.

On the other hand, we find many authors who consider it necessary to respond to the needs of the different kinds of children and show us the different types of teaching which may be the most appropriate depending on the nature of the person and on the different types of intelligence.

> We know through the work of Paul Torrance, David Holb, Honey and Mumford, Daniel Goleman and Howard Gardner that people respond positively to different learning stimuli; but despite progress there is still much work to do to help organisations, whether they are schools, further or higher education establishments or places of employment, become somewhere that individuals enthusiastically want to attend (Thorne 2007: 87).

As teachers, we must promote creativity in the classroom. We have to be a bit odd and eccentric, we should carry out different and funny activities with our pupils, walk barefoot or wearing our pullover inside out. Tales and stories give us a great opportunity to present creativity in the classroom, to give wings to children's imagination.

Take a story like *Kate Morag and the Wedding*, written by Mairie Hedderwick, which takes place on an island in Scotland. At the beginning, it seems to be incomprehensible. Who had the idea to create a story where a grandmother decides to celebrate a wedding and the other grandmother, whose old boyfriend comes back after years of absence and takes her for a tour ( by helicopter!)? The book acts as a wonderful springboard to carry out a CLIL workshop using the *Mantle of the Expert technique* designed by Dorothy Heathcote. We adopt the plan proposed by Wyse and Dowson (2009) and the class becomes the island. Around Katie we realize multiple activities for the students and each one may choose the activity he prefers to develop, the one which is closer to his personality, skills and interests.

We take into account Gardner's *Multiple Intelligences* theory where he differentiates between:

1.   Linguistic intelligence
2.   Logical-mathematical intelligence
3.   Musical intelligence
4.   Spatial intelligence
5.   Bodily-kinaesthetic intelligence
6.   Interpersonal intelligence
7.   Intrapersonal intelligence

As each student develops in a different rhythm, in this way we respond to the needs of all the children and all of them can feel fulfilled. So we wonder, who will write the invitations and the menu for the wedding feast? The one who possesses linguistic intelligence. Who will be the postman who organizes letter? A child who has logical-mathematical intelligence. Who will compose the fanfare for the bride or the music for the dance? A child who has musical intelligence. Who will draw the map of the island based on the children's interpretation of the story? A child who has spatial intelligence. Who will play the grandmother's boyfriend who flies the helicopter or the postman who cycles all over the island visiting the neighbours? A child who has bodily-kinaesthetic intelligence.

In short, moving away from the traditional approach to literature, where a story was told and the children were asked for a summary and an analysis of characters, we pursue more ambitious aims. It is the children who star in the story, who give life to the characters. They develop, interact with the others, and solve problems. They do not summarize but expand the story and they may even change the end if they wish.

Authors like Sperry and Ornstein focus on the right and left brain hemispheres and how they are linked with different skills and abilities. On the right hemisphere we find rhythm, colour, imagination, daydreaming, intuition, spatial awareness and music. On the left we find logic, lists, linear, words, numbers, sequence and analysis.

| *Left brain* | *Right brain* |
|---|---|
| Logic | Rhythm |
| Lists | Colour |
| Linear | Imagination |
| Words | Daydreaming |
| Numbers | Intuition |
| Sequence | Spatial awareness |
| Analysis | Music |

Figure 4.1. Functions of brain hemispheres. (Ornstein 1974)

So students with dominant right hemisphere would be responsible for preparing the hall, elaborating the garlands and decorating the wedding cake – made of modelling clay – and those with prevalent left hemisphere could write the list of guests, set the price of the menu in the restaurants of the island or write the information leaflet for the helicopter tour Kate's grandmother's enjoys.

The *Mantle of the Expert* technique as a vehicle to develop creativity in the child is suitable because it is an open and flexible activity where all the abilities and skills can be integrated, not only intellectual but also motor skills, in such a way that everybody will feel fulfilled when participating in this workshop. Plenty of times we find students who have a special gift for music or drama, but there are also many others whom we cannot see. Sometimes in the fast pace of the class, it is not easy to look for a space and a time for them to show their art and share it with their classmates.

When we use the *Mantle of the Expert* technique, we plan in advance a session of several hours where we set a dramatic context. Students are given some time to adapt to this new way of working, to believe in it, feel confident and lose their inhibition, so they can develop their role of *expert*. The classroom becomes a channel of creativity and authenticity where teachers do not create the rules but each pupil freely and spontaneously makes his original contribution to this fictitious world. *Mantle* technique turns into an enriching activity enabling children the responsibility to grow as individuals.

## Drama in foreign language teaching

In the thirties in Great Britain and USA, a trend starts where drama companies visit schools and present their plays to children – companies such as *Fen Players, Playmates* or *Junior Programs Inc.* After the war these companies came back led by powerful figures like Peter Slade or Brian Way, who developed *Theatre-in-Education* or *TIE* to use drama techniques with educative aims. *Belgrade Theatre,* in the city of Coventry (United Kingdom), is the theatre where the first group of teachers-actors was trained, and it promoted the creation of many others. In 1986, the group declared as their main aim to present complex drama conflicts that children should solve through questions and decision making. Ideas which would link with those of the actress and teacher trainer Dorothy Heathcote who published her essential *Drama for learning* (1967, 1994). The techniques used by *TIE* have been an enormous influence in the development of children and youth drama in Great Britain and in modern education. She developed resources such as *teacher-in-role* where the teacher/actor addresses the audience to ask for some advice about acting and *hotseating,* where the audience asks the characters.

In North America there was also a huge interest in the use of drama in Education. Winifred Ward, professor from Northwestern University in Evanston (Illinois), distinguishes between *creative dramatics*, making reference to the ludic and educative activities, realized at school through drama and *children's theatre,* which refers to drama as an aesthetical activity. Other authors like Geraldine Siks (1958) and Nellie

McCaslin (1968) from the University of New York, have also written about the use of drama in education.

Since the publication of books like *Handbook for Teaching* in 1937, there was a great interest in training teachers in the use of drama activities in Great Britain. From the 50s and 60s, writers such as Peter Slade (1954), Brian Kay (1967), Dorothy Heathcote (1967) or Gavin Bolton (1979) researched about drama in education and its possibilities to be exploited in the national curriculum. Similarly, the Canadian Richard Courtney (1968) qualifies educative drama, the *total experience,* as a discipline which includes all branches of knowledge. He indicates that the role of the teacher will be to help students in their personal fulfilment.

While some authors like Slade (1978), Heathcote (1967), Courtney (1968) or Bolton (1979) have stated that the main objective of drama in education is the intellectual, social and emotional development of students, others like Moffett (1967), Seely (1976) and O'Neill and Lambert (1988) consider drama as an ideal resource for the acquisition and development of linguistic skills. Pérez Gutiérrez (2004) presents drama as the most perfect technique for the development of linguistic skills. Likewise, O'Neill and Lambert (1988) say that the most important contribution drama gives to education is to provide a suitable environment for the development of several kinds of language. Through the realization of drama activities, students develop and acquire communicative competences and basic attitudes towards the world which surrounds them. Drama activities stimulate creation of language and the assimilation of linguistic models.

From the publication of the manual of *Drama Techniques in Language Learning* by Maley and Duff in 1978, many other works on the use of drama activities in the foreign language class have been published. The book presents a compilation of more than a hundred activities to carry out in the English class. Later, a revised edition entitled *Drama Techniques in Language Learning. A resource book of communication activities for language teachers* (1982) would expand introductory techniques, observation interpretation, creation and invention, wordplay, problem solving, the use of literary texts, poems, songs and a day's work. Maley's book is based on his long experience using drama techniques in the English classroom. It includes a wide selection of activities which provide authentic reasons to express feelings and personal opinions. Intellect seldom functions without an emotional element, however teaching materials very often lack it. Maley (1978) states that many of the skills we need when we speak a foreign language are not considered when elaborating text books, such as adaptability (the ability to match one's speech to the person one is talking to), speed of reaction, sensitivity to tone, insight, anticipation, in short, appropriateness. People we face every day are not flat characters and not all of them have such common names such as Smith or Brown. People may be happy or angry, tired or worried. They may speak fast or slowly, and they may repeat phrases. But this is the interesting thing; they are alive.

Drama tries to give this emotional content which has been forgotten back to language. That is to say, we have to pay attention to meaning. Alan Maley states that linguistic structure has to be taught always and from the beginning with meaning. Regarding the role of the teacher, he "sues how some foreign language teachers behave like the owners of language estates, putting up high walls round their territory and signs saying 'No trespassin'" (1978: 10). The activities Maley proposes make us take life as a starting point: situations and daily conflicts. Drama includes a wide range of aspects such as music, history, painting and maths: "Drama is like the naughty child who climbed the high walls and ignores the 'no trespassing' signs, skiing, photography, cooking" (Maley: 1978: 10). There are no barriers. Just then, when children find out that there is a world beyond the shrivelled characters who live in the textbooks, Peter, Jane, Mary, they will start to feel really interested.

To be able to use these drama techniques successfully, it is essential to make a radical change in the relationship between teacher and students. These activities cannot work unless there is a relaxed atmosphere in the classroom. The main function of the teacher will be to set things in motion, and be sure that students understand what we want them to do.

*Teacher training*

After having reviewed some theories related to the use of drama in education and when it is time to draw conclusions, everything leads us to the figure of the teacher, to the role that he/she plays in this new approach to language teaching. The teacher must support students in all their statements, giving a greater priority to fluency than to accuracy in the language used.

In Spain, the adoption of the Anglo-Saxon model should be adjusted to a different reality. Educational context and differences in the curriculum are clearly displayed between both countries. For example, music is essential for the complete development of children in United Kingdom and Ireland. Children from the very beginning receive vocal training. They are taught music and how to play an instrument. However, in Spain, most of the times music is conceived just as one more subject and only those children who join a choir or study in a school of music are the ones who learn to sing.

*Dorothy Heathcote:* The Mantle of the Expert *approach.*

Mantle of the Expert: *definition*

First of all I have to express my belief that drama, role-play and simulation play an essential role when developing creativity. The technique named *Mantle of the Expert,* designed in the 1980s by Dorothy Heathcote, a drama teacher and later lecturer at the University of Newcastle-upon-Tyne, uses an approach to learning known as *Community of Research,* where children are responsible for running an enterprise in a fictitious world. Heathcote has trained many generations of English and American teachers. She proposes the teacher-in-role as a participant who lives the educative problem. Dorothy's technique consists of posing a conflict over which children have to think to be able to solve. It is in this process of debate, negotiation and acting, where the enormous pedagogic potential of drama lies.

In this technique, drama is used as a starting point for a pedagogy based upon the belief that children learn better when they feel motivated and involved in their task and children are treated as if they were experts in a particular field. This technique requires that teachers cease to rely on their memories and their knowledge, and instead, rely on what they are, where they are in their thinking and how they communicate their ideas rather than what they say to their students via the traditional conversations which form such a large part of our school and college systems. They metaphorically wear the mantle of the expert in a context which provides the basis for learning. Children are engaged with different tasks in the classroom such as reading, sorting of information, writing, arts and crafts, maths… just the type of activities students are invited to do by every teacher.

The use of the *Mantle of the Expert* technique offers us not only a vast world of creative possibilities but also a particular occasion for children to develop their imagination and empathy. Life in a Mediaeval Monastery? Sceptical teachers may wonder how a nine-year-old child can be interested in the way monks live in the medieval epoch. The Bishop Letter? Children do not even know what a bishop is, they cannot write a proper letter. Too complex! A Monastery Floor Plan? They absolutely ignore this issue!

However, reality is far different. We have to trust children and never undervalue them. That is what Heathcote thought in designing and putting into practice the *Mantle of the Expert* approach across the curriculum. In her book *Drama for Learning* (1994) she presents the technique introducing us to life in a mediaeval monastery where she involves children in its running in medieval times. The argument put forward by Dorothy Heathcote is "that because the students are to be in role in a fictional context, they will bring a sense of responsibility to their learning, with the result that the teacher is able, through the drama, to make greater demands on the students than if this alternative trigger to learning were missing" (Heathcote, D. & G. Bolton 1994: 48).

*Role of the teacher*

Regarding the role of the teacher in Heathcote's mind, to be an excellent teacher means to see students as they are, without labels or stereotypes. It means taking a risk, leaving aside the traditional role which is more comfortable and fully participating in the process of learning. It means pushing yourself and your pupils to the limits of their capacities – the teacher participates in the class aiming to establish with his pupils the shared experiences through subtlety and challenging their traditions.

Although Dorothy was continuously teaching children, most of her time was devoted to teacher training and proposing alternative ideas for the courses taught in the School of Education of Newcastle. This was due to the fact that she did not agree with the traditional teacher training programmes which were designed to widen the knowledge of university students without giving the same priority to the transfer of this academic learning into practice in the classroom. According to Heathcote, we could define a teacher as one who creates situations of learning for the others. A teacher's reward comes because this energy flows in the two directions. It is a return ticket.

*Guidelines*

Regarding the guidelines proposed by Heathcote, teachers have to take into account the following to present the *Mantle of the Expert*.
–   Preparation: drama context has to be presented in an effective way.
–   Fiction: specific language structures which show we are in a fictitious reality must be used, such as *Suppose that...; if we could...; If people would let us...; I bet If we tried we could...*
–   Dynamics of action: the frame of action has to be presented in a clear and direct way.
–   A past history and an implied future: children participate in a specific event. They have to know all about it, what has happened before and what is expected to happen afterwards, to be able to develop the task successfully.

## Practical experience

Romance has been brewing on the island between Neilly Beag and Granma Mainland and everyone is thrilled when they announce that they are to be

married. Everyone, that is, except Grannie Island. For some reason that Katie
Morag can't fathom her island grandmother is not happy at all (Hedderwick
1995: 27).

At the beginning of the course I always ask students to write an auto-
biography in English about their background, knowledge of the foreign
language and also about their hobbies and interests, and it has to end
with the sentence: "and the most remarkable feature of my personality
is…". This activity is very useful because it gives me information about
their standard of English and it also helps me to design activities and to
make work groups.

The following workshop reconciles CLIL with Arts and Crafts,
taking as a starting point a children's literature book, *Katie Morag and
the Wedding* by Mairi Hedderwick, inspired by Dominic Wyse and Pam
Dowson's (2009) proposal. It is a story which takes place on a Scottish
Island where one of Katie's grandmother is getting married. This is the
plot. In the class we perform the whole story, playing the different characters – main and secondary- who appear in the book.

The story begins in a post office building. There is much activity.
Customers send letters, receive parcels, make phone calls, buy enve-
lopes and stamps. Also, the postmen prepare their mailbags and start
delivering. After reading the book, students have to choose the character they are now performing, or better, living! They are on their worksite
and have started their tasks. I, of course, stop my role as teacher and
also participate in the story. I choose to become a customer who must
make a phone call to a friend. I live the role. Likewise, students play
their role and become involved in the story. They forget they are performing. I ask them to adopt other sexes and ages and I suggest they act
individually and also in groups, so we find loving couples, a family with
twin children, etc. Once the context is established, a range of activities
follow. There are different tables with activities from which students can
choose. They include the following:

•     Inventing a board game based on the story.
•     Creating maps of the island based on the children's interpreta-
      tions of the story or from the book's endpapers.
•     Composing some music for the wedding celebration.

- Writing postcards.
- Creating a menu for the café on the island.
- Designing wedding invitations.
- Writing letters between the two grannies.
- Making a menu for the wedding party.
- Writing something to go on the village notice board.
- Making small cakes and decorating them like a wedding cake.
- Making wedding decorations.
- Making a plan for the wedding, outlining the events of the day so everyone knows where to be, and for what!
- Designing a leaflet for a helicopter flight over the island.

The time comes when we have to prepare the Wedding Hall. I have gathered information from reading the autobiographies and I name a student–who seems adequate for the role–as Decoration Manager, whose task was to decorate the hall. The result was amazing. She was really an expert. She prepared flowers with tissue paper, made delicate garlands for the walls and made an impressive wedding cake. She showed her skills as artist and designer. Other students were cooks. They made *delicious* recipes with modelling clay. They were involved in the activity discussing the different shapes, sizes and tastes.

The time for the religious ceremony came. I already knew one of the students had studied Music and I asked her to bring the violin to the class. She was choosing tunes to accompany different points in the ceremony. She started to play the soundtrack of the film *The Mission* by Ennio Morricone. It was such beautiful music that all of us were really touched. She was an expert. The rest of the students had not studied music and nobody else was able to play an instrument. The pupil felt proud when we applauded her performance. Later, in the ceremony, she played the *Pirates of the Caribbean* tune and filled the event with joy and magic.

This activity, carried out by English student teachers, may be adapted for children, encouraging them to adopt those roles which are appropriate for them. Sometimes children are shy and it is hard for them to show their abilities. But one of the most surprising revelations I found was the reaction of the students when I, the teacher, was involved in the story. We were in the Church after the priest had blessed the bride and the bridegroom and I asked them to kiss each other, clapped my hands and the other students joined in. The bride and the bridegroom were bewildered, they were thinking the teacher was crazy and they were really embarrassed, despite of the fact that the bridegroom was thirty years old!

The same scene took place in a *restaurant*. We were having dinner at a wedding where they had designed the invitations. They had written the menu and had decorated the hall. We were really celebrating Katie's Grandmother's wedding. But there were still more surprises in the story. An old man, the missing boyfriend of the other grandmother, turned up. And there was the student pilot describing the sky from his helicopter (chair).

We lived this reality in the class, postmen running because they were late, post office employees working with their toy tills to get the price of the product, customers waiting patiently or (some) impatiently in queues, designers and illustrators, decoration managers, cooks, waiters serving the wine and the different dishes, the priest giving his improvised homily, tourist agents designing the itinerary for the honeymoon. Thirty people *living* their role, having fun or getting angry or sad because they haven't been invited to the event. The whole group was living a unique and unforgettable experience, enjoying the pretence, the illusion, suspension of disbelief, or as Dorothy Heathcote would say *the big lie*; speaking English, living in English, being experts in various skills.

I think one of the most important elements to make students believe in the story, be involved in the wedding, forget it is an English class, is the fact that the teacher has played the same game. There is a risk. They may think the teacher is a bit weird, but who cares? It is such a small price that I am happy to pay if in this way I can teach my students, show them that they are also able to do it, and that they will be able to do the same in the future when they work with children in the English class.

In line with Dorothy Heathcote's thoughts: Do we need a space with a specific size for my class? No, as long as it has a roof. Do we need special materials? No, just some pencils, some sheets of paper and a pair of scissors. How many people can participate? Everybody. What age? It is not relevant. This is possible when we have our own energy and creativity. We do not need any external help.

Dorothy Heathcote warns us that maybe the teacher/technician threatens to replace the teacher/artist and maybe society which already undervalues good teachers. Creativity in teaching will allow the quest for excellence and effort for quality in teaching extinguishes. This possibility leads us to the main objective of her teaching and writing which is to seek to challenge, shatter and reform ideas.

We definitely agree with Johnson and O'Neill's belief that it may not be possible to imitate with the same success her style of teaching but it is possible to learn from her skills and experience to join her in the demand for better and more vigorous and relevant teacher training. This will produce committed young teachers capable of pursuing excellence and authenticity in our schools (1984). The first step may be to create a suitable environment, decorating the cold walls of the classroom which – as the white walls of the hospital or the dark bars of the prison – do silence our imagination, shorten our freedom and make impossible the development of creativity. That is a bright idea but not all the teachers are ready for the development of creativity in the world of teaching.

## Conclusions

Concluding these ideas on the way of awakening students' creativity through different techniques with the aim of improving learning, CLIL and drama show a lot of connections in the process of teaching and learning:

- The teacher has to leave his role of authority and pull down the wall which separates him from the students.
- He has to stop being an observer. He has to be close, accessible and participate in the educative experience with pupils.
- He has to help to create the relaxed atmosphere necessary to carry out the *Mantle* technique.
- We have to enter into a suspension of disbelief. The teacher has to act within the story which is built by the whole group, where each person chooses his role and his responsibility; each one

carries out his corresponding tasks and really this is about living an exciting experience where once they have accepted the game and its rules, actors are fully involved in the situation. They flow with the story and they speak English, maybe with some grammatical mistakes or some word mispronounced but the most important thing is the fact that students interact, ask questions and answers and offer solutions. It is relevant that they may express their creativity in the field they find more attractive according to their abilities and interests.

•   A teacher has to be an artist, at least at the beginning, while students accept this change in the process of learning. The teacher has to be the liveliest guest in the party, the customer who complains loudest in the queue in the post office, the chef who chooses the most delicious ingredients for the menu or the postman who spends more time in the delivery of parcels.

Maybe students are not used to this function. As it happened in the *Katie* experience, where students seemed to be really puzzled when I got involved in that world of fiction. At the beginning it was hard for them to enter into the story, believe in their characters, but at the end of the session I think the result was much better than expected. Students could display all their creativity in different ways. They expressed themselves, developing their skills, their gifts and for some hours, when we decorated the ceiling with garlands, made a toast with plastic glasses, listened to music and danced around the bridegroom, we *were* the guests invited to the wedding feast in the island of Stray.

Welcome to the *Mantle of the Expert* technique where each student finds his tone, his voice. Welcome you, teacher, for being accomplice in this adventure.

## References

Aymerich, C. & M. 1974. *Expresión y arte en la escuela [Expression and Art at School]*. Barcelona: Teide.

Bolton, G. 1979. *Towards a Theory of Drama in Education*. London: Longman.

Buzan, T. 2001. *Head Strong*. London: Thorsons, 2001.

Cook, C. 1917. *The Play Way*. London: Heinemann.

Courtney, R. 1968. *Play, Drama and Thought*. London: Cassell & Co.Ltd.

Coyle, D. / Hood, P. / Marsh, D. 2010. *CLIL. Content and Language Integrated Learning*. Cambridge: CUP.

Gardner, H. 1993. *Frames of Mind*. New York: Basic Books.

____. 2006. *Multiple Intelligences*. New York: Basic Books.

Goleman, D. 1998. *Working with Emotional Intelligence*. London: Bloomsbury.

Heathcote, D. / Bolton, G. 1994. *Drama for Learning*. Portsmouth: Heinemann.

Hedderwick, M. 1995. *Katie Morag and the Wedding*. London: Red Fox.

Jenkins, H. (ed).1993. *The Arden Shakespeare. Hamlet*. London & New York: Routledge.

Johnson, L. / O'Neill, C. (eds). 1991. *Collected Writings on Education and Drama. Dorothy Heathcote*. Evanston, Illinois: Northwestern University Press.

Maley, A. / Duff, A. 1978. *Drama Techniques in Language Learning*. Cambridge: CUP.

____. 1982. *Drama Techniques in Language Learning. A resource book of communication activities for language teachers*. Cambridge: CUP.

McCaslin, N. 1984. *Creative Drama in the Classroom*. New York: Longman.

Moffett, J. 1967. *Drama: What is Happening? The Use of Dramatic Activities en the Teaching of English*. Illinois: National Council of Teachers of English.

Norton, D. 1993. *Through the Eyes of a Child. An Introduction to Children's literature*. London: Prentice-Hall.

O'Neill, C. / Lambert, A. 1982. *Drama Structures: A Practical Handbook for Teachers*. London: Hutchinson.

Ornstein, R. (ed). 1974. *Nature of Human Consciousness* (A Book of Readings). New York: Viking Adult.

O'Toole, J. 1976. *Theatre – in- Education*. London: Hodder & Stought-
on.
Pérez, M. 2004. La dramatización como recurso clave en el proceso de
enseñanza y adquisición de las lenguas [Drama as key resource
in the process of teaching and acquisition of languages]. *Glosas
Didácticas* 12/Autumn, 70–80.
Seely, J. 1976. *In Context: Language and Drama in the Secondary
School*. Oxford: OUP.
Siks, G. B. 1958. *Creative Dramatics: An Art for Children*. New York:
Harper & Row.
Slade, P. 1978. *Expresión dramática infantil [Children Drama Expres-
sion]*. Madrid: Aula XXI Santillana.
Thorne, K. 2007. *Essential Creativity in the Classroom. Inspiring Kids*.
London & New York: Routledge.
Torrance, P. 1962. *Guiding Creative Talent*. Upper Saddle River, NJ:
Prentice Hall.
_____. 2002. *Manifesto: A Guide to Developing a Creative Career*.
Westport, CT: Ablex.
Way, B. 1967. *Development through Drama*. London: Longman.
Wyse, D. / Dowson, P. 2009. *The Really Useful Creativity Book*. London
& New York: Routledge.

Nailya Garipova

# Linking theatre to CLIL in Secondary Schools: Bilingual Plays

> A play in English is a success. We all need successes, for these encourage us to strive for further success (Richard Via).

## Introduction

A growing number of studies focused on the content and language integration (CLIL) has been recently conducted in the field of teaching foreign languages. The fundamental principal of CLIL is to serve a double purpose: to help students develop their target language skills through a linguistic immersion and make the target language a tool to learn other school subjects.

This chapter explores the advantages of using theatre in a CLIL approach. Theatre is an excellent pedagogical resource for exploring the theoretical and practical aspects of a foreign language teaching. It is a very useful tool for the CLIL methodology too. The combination of theatre and CLIL offers a different approach in the teaching of a foreign language in Spain, since most of the teaching is based on a course textbook. Both theatre and CLIL break with the traditional classroom routine of working with the texts, such as reading, listening, answering questions or doing grammar and vocabulary exercises. As Drew (2003) points out, "CLIL provides the context for using the target language functionally to learn about something else". Theatre becomes the tool for communicating that something else.

The type of theatre proposed here is aware of the reality of our pupils and enables teachers to adopt a communicative approach in foreign language teaching according to the CLIL methodology. Here we propose the *teatro de entorno*[1] recommended by Juan José Torres Nunez (1996). The objective is to create the working atmosphere needed to stimulate the pupils' motivation and cooperation. With the implementation of this kind of theatre in the classroom we propose the following specific objectives of teaching-learning, based on the principles developed by Torres Nuñez (1996: 40–45):

1.   To adapt a bilingual play to the socio-cultural context of the pupils and to show how such a play can be created.
2.   To promote the coexistence of languages and cultures.
3.   To provide the pupils with a real communication.
4.   To develop the five basic competences: linguistic competence, learning to learn, social and citizenship competence, competence in mathematics, digital and information processing competence, cultural and artistic competence, autonomy competence, and the competence in the knowledge about and interacting with the environment.
5.   To use theatre as a motivational tool in the foreign language classroom.
6.   To help the pupils to understand accents of different non-native English speakers.
7.   To develop the pupils' imagination and creative power.
8.   To understand the pupils' reality and to promote their cooperation with the teachers.
9.   To introduce learning CCTs.

## Theatre and CLIL in foreign language teaching

Using theatre in foreign language methodology is one of the most studied and exploited strategies in the classroom. Although many studies have been conducted on this topic, here we are going to mention only those we consider important for our proposal. For example, Alan Maley

---

1    J.J. Torres Nuñez (1996: 44) used the term "teatro de entorno" to refer to a kind of theatre rooted in the socio-cultural setting of the students.

and Alan Duff (1982) enumerate the benefits of using theatre techniques in the foreign language classroom. Sam (1990) comments on the pedagogical value of theatre in teaching and identifies main advantages and disadvantages of its use. Kao (1998) points out the qualities the teacher must have in order to implement theatre successfully. Juan Jose Torres Nuñez (1996 and 1997) shows the pedagogical value of theatre in the classroom. Apart from establishing a theoretical framework for theatre in the foreign language teaching, this author also created bilingual English-Spanish plays for Spanish students with staging instructions. Susana Nicolás Roman (2011) published an article where she proposed to use theatre to develop the basic competences of the students. The recent contribution of Anna Corral Fullá (2013) discusses various theatre practices in the language classroom and analyses one of the primary teaching materials designed for teaching Spanish as a foreign language. Web materials are also worth commenting since the Internet offers a wide range of drama and plays in English.

All these authors consider theatre a universal and integrating resource. To them, theatre offers many advantages for the language classroom. Above all, it enhances development of the basic competences, as we have stated in the objectives proposed. It helps the learner to acquire new vocabulary and structures in a fully contextualized and integrated manner (Wessels, 1987); it serves to improve students' pronunciation and intonation (Smith, 1984 and Wessels, 1987). When acting, students learn to link language to other forms of communication, like gesture, facial expressions, body language; and they increase their fluency (Hayes, 1984: 9). Theatre is a well-known motivating tool as well (Boudreau, 2010 and Burke & O'Sullivan, 2002). Furthermore, it has a positive effect on "classroom dynamics and atmosphere, thus facilitating the formation of a bonded group which learns together" (Maley and Duff, 2005: 67). It helps to overcome shyness and the lack of self-esteem (Hardison & Sonchaeng, 2005).

Despite the pedagogical power of theatre (Torres Núñez, 1996), it has been scarcely exploited in the foreign language classroom in Spain. This is due to the problems that teachers have to face in their schools. One of the biggest problems is the lack of an appropriate material. As a rule, secondary school libraries have drama sketches, role-plays and readers. But these are usually used as mere graded readers. Drama sketches do not have many characters; this creates many difficulties if we want to work with a large group in the classroom. Although theatre companies such as *Face to Face* or *IPA Productions* have appeared lately, we should bear in mind that most of these plays are either written by native English authors or adapted from the classic plays. In any case, as a rule, they do not correlate with the students' linguistic level nor with their socio-cultural background.

Most of secondary school textbooks for learning English present drama tasks, among which two types can be distinguished: open-dramatization tasks and those supervised by teachers. In open-drama tasks students create their own dialogues having simple instructions as a starting point. Whereas in supervised tasks these instructions include particular linguistic structures that students must use to create their dialogues. Although both types of drama tasks require creation and staging of a particular communicative situation, they also share the same disadvantage: they do not always appeal to the students, as generally, they deal with outdated topics (this problem is increasing if we take into account that secondary school pupils have to study with the same textbooks for more than eight years due to the policy of free textbooks in Spanish secondary schools).

The difficulty concerning suitable material becomes even more evident if we consider the last instructions and recommendations elaborated by the Andalucian regional government (June, 19, 2013) for bilingual schools. According to the current legislation, authorized bilingual schools must offer bilingual education with the CLIL approach, using their own materials or those provided by the Andalucian regional government. These materials should promote students' active participation and develop the four communicative skills: listening, reading, writing and speaking. However, the so-called "recommended" materials for the bilingual education exclude theatre.

In foreign language teaching, the pedagogical value of theatre and drama is obvious. They also seem useful for the CLIL approach. Over the last years, CLIL has become a well-established part of the education system in Spain. The CLIL methodology focuses on learning that requires an acquisition of concepts, skills and attitudes. As stated in the Royal Decree 231/ 2007 and in the Order from June 28, 2011, the specific objectives of the bilingual schools programme are the following (quoted from Casal and Moore, 2009):

1.  The learning of some content areas will be carried out in a language other than the L1.
2.  The methodology implemented at secondary levels will be based on communication, interaction by means of language immersion and the balanced development of oral and written skills.
3.  From a linguistic point of view, the goal is general skills development embracing the L1 as well as the L2, and at later stages an L3. This implies not only an increase in partial linguistic competences in different languages but also the development of a pan-linguistic consciousness.
4.  Learners will be confronted with different codes which will lead them to reflect upon linguistic behaviour. This approach should foster a special development of learners' metacognitive skills and a natural use of languages as distinct from an explicit knowledge of linguistic codes.
5.  Students will manipulate language in relation to different areas and academic content, multiplying the contexts wherein they will be able to efficiently use languages linked to academic and professional fields.
6.  Students will need to manipulate diverse linguistic codes in order to 'do things', developing cognitive flexibility towards analysis and observation of learning processes.
7.  From a cultural viewpoint, students in bilingual sections will be in touch with other realities at an early age, being able to draw comparisons with their own surroundings and increasing their interest in different cultures with different traditions, customs, institutions and techniques.

As different authors have stated (Lagabaster and Ruiz de Zarobe, 2010; Juan Rubio and García Conesa, 2012, and Bret Blasco, 2012, among the others), CLIL teaching may open doors to a student-centred, function-focused, task-oriented, authentic and constructivist classroom; it may even serve as a means of promoting learner autonomy. To quote Baetens Beardsmore, "it would appear that bilingual skills lead to greater development of creativity both on verbal and non-verbal levels of activity" (2008: 6).

Leaving theoretical considerations apart, in bilingual Secondary Schools in Spain, we can face a different reality. Depending on the methodological approach taken and the teaching materials used, CLIL classes can also be turned into a less valuable experience when dealing with traditional, repetition targeted, form focused on exercises. Furthermore, according to Susan Hillyard (2010), "CLIL deals with subject areas or content which can sometimes be dry and technical, even when practiced by an experienced teacher".

As Drew (2013) suggests, "theatre research into CLIL has shown that the approach leads to both affective and cognitive aims on learners". There is a connection between CLIL and theatre that can be beneficial for educational purposes in many perspectives. According to Muszynska (2012: 237), the connection between these two mainly consists of two aspects. On the one hand, they are both seen as motivating forces in the language classroom. On the other, they are both characterized by a holistic nature that engages the whole learner in the learning experience. Hillyard (2010) identified the following benefits of combing theatre to CLIL:

> The benefits of CLIL may be seen in terms of cultural awareness, internalization, language competence, preparation for life itself, study and working life, and, most crucially of all, increased motivation through the development of the person as a whole, not just a language learner. The joy of putting CLIL together with drama is that all of those elements are magnified producing a dynamic, effective and enjoyable learning experience for all.

Having established that both theatre and CLIL are equally relevant in current education and that both lead to affective and cognitive gains in learners, the aim of the following section is to show how the two of them can be combined in foreign language teaching.

## Towards a different type of theatre for the CLIL approach: bilingual plays

As stated before, the type of theatre proposed here is aware of the reality of our pupils. It also contributes to the meaningful learning, key aim in the CLIL approach. It stimulates the pupils' motivation as it combines such techniques as creation and repetition. This type of theatre fulfils the following principles (developed from the principles provided by Wessels, 1987 and Torres Nuñez, 1996):

1.  Students will adapt a bilingual play to their socio-cultural surrounding. Then, they will create an original play. Teacher will supervise the creation of the play and correct its final draft.
2.  All the students of the group can take part in the adaptation and elaboration of the plays. They will choose the parts voluntarily.
3.  One or more Spanish speaking characters (who will not speak any English) will be introduced in the play in order to create misunderstanding.
4.  These plays will reflect local socio-cultural setting of the students. The Spanish characters will speak with the local accent. The introduction of the Spanish speaking characters will help listeners to understand and follow the play; it will also serve as practice for students whose mother tongue is not Spanish.
5.  The theme of the play should be interesting and amusing and must be chosen by the pupils.
6.  The play should be written in contemporary English, without witty puns.
7.  The lexical richness should correlate with the contents of the syllabus.
8.  There should be as many characters as possible in the play.
9.  The play must have female and male characters.
10. Apart from dialogues, there must be action.
11. The sets should be simple. Bearing in mind school's budget, school material should be used when possible.
12. The play should be either one-act play or a very short-full length one (30–60 minutes).

When adapting and creating our bilingual plays, *teatro de entorno*, these criteria were followed.


## Classroom implementations


Our bilingual theatre project started in February 2011 and went on until the writing of this article (April 2014). The setting is a state secondary school in Albox, in the Almeria province. At the beginning, it was a part of the school project carried out within the CLIL track. Two years ago, this original activity was included in the Reading Promotion Plan implemented by the regional government of Andalusia. As regards the practical background of the proposal, it is designed for the second cycle of Secondary Compulsory Education (3º–4º ESO), for pupils aged 14–16.

The idea of using theatre had its origin when I had to teach English in the bilingual group of the third year of Compulsory Secondary Education and I was the CLIL project coordinator of our school. The group was quite heterogeneous; there were pupils from nine different nationalities. As a teacher, I faced the problem of cultural co-existence among the pupils, as some of them made up inflexible groups according to their nationality and did not mix with the rest of the class (this happened with British students and Pakistani girls). The level of English was heterogeneous as well, and it was not all the students' foreign language or L2 (being the mother tongue for the British pupils and a second foreign language for the pupils from Asia and East of Europe). English was a shared communicative tool among the pupils of this group. After having obtained the results of the first term and analyzed the problems of the group I decided to use theatre to increase cooperation and to improve the learning process. I believe that new, innovative and non-traditional activities often appeal to students in the foreign language classroom.

The first play that was adapted and staged by this group was *The Barber of Almeria*, written by Torres Nuñez (1997). Although the students worked with other plays in the following years, and taking into account that the methodology of implementing different plays is similar, I am going to illustrate how we worked with this play.

The first thing we did was to read the play in class. This reading activity is a good option to be introduced in the weekly reading sessions (as stated by the *Instructions from June 11, 2012* and *Instructions from June 23, 2013 for the Andalusian Secondary Schools*). When reading the play, we provided the students with while-reading activities to work on the unknown vocabulary and grammar structures. Then the adaptation of the play took place. We changed the original title *The Barber of Almeria*, for *The Barber of Albox* and substituted proper names that appeared in the text (the characters' names and the names of places were adapted to our setting). We modified dialogues in Spanish, introducing the expressions from the local speech. We added five characters more (at the end there were 14 characters in the play) and added one extra-scene. After that, the students chose their parts and began to learn them. The rest of the pupils were in charge of sets and the stage props. They searched for pictures of people from different nationalities on the Internet; then, in the sessions of drawing, they drew portraits of the people to decorate the hairdresser's. Other students were responsible for looking for the suitable furniture to decorate the stage. Several pupils were in charge of video recording and taking pictures during rehearsals and the final performance. In this way, the students without parts became active listeners.

When rehearsing and staging the play, we had the opportunity to exploit its linguistic contents. The pictures the students drew were used in warm-up activities to practice vocabulary related to people's appearance, parts of the body and clothing. Students were also provided with information and extra-practice on intonation. Some of the grammar structures that appeared in the play were explained and reinforced with practical exercises. Foreign pupils had an opportunity to learn expressions from the local speech, the so-called "Albojense". It was fun to hear Spanish students teach their foreign classmates how to pronounce typical expressions of their hometown. Students could also listen to different non-native English speakers speak English. Some of the tasks derived from the play were proposed to enhance students' intercultural communicative competence. For example, some of the sessions were

devoted to the study of body language of people from different nationalities; in other lessons, the foreign students made presentations on ce-
lebrities of their countries. In the sessions of computer science students
learnt how to give PowerPoint presentations, using photos and videos
they recorded during the play's performance. In the Spanish language
sessions, students were provided with tasks to work on formal and in-
formal registers of the Spanish language.

As to the timing, it took three months to carry out the activity. At
the beginning, the play was read in the sessions devoted to the Reading
promotion (once a week). Then, the students rehearsed the play in the
sessions of English workshop under the supervision of the language
assistant. Some of the rehearsals were introduced as warm-ups in the
sessions of the English language, whereas the final rehearsals took
place in the evenings. The play was performed in the Intercultural Festi-
val, which is celebrated every year, for the school students and teachers.
After the successful performance, we were invited to put the same play
on again, in the concert-hall of the town-hall. Then, it was not the usual
school play.

As has been mentioned, the activity was carried out during the
second term. Using this kind of theatre was my way to solve the problems of this particular group. During the third term I could see that with
the implementation of the bilingual theatre, the communication and
cooperation among the students from different nationalities improved
considerably. Most of the students improved their pronunciation and
fluency in English, whereas some foreign pupils seemed to be more
motivated to learn Spanish as a L2.

We also provided the students and their families with questionnaires to get their feedback of the theatre project. The results were
positive and most of the parents encouraged us to continue with our
work. As a result, during the following years, bilingual plays adapted
from those written by Torres Nuñez were also used in other groups of
our school.

After having adapted and staged different plays, my students of
the fourth year of Compulsory Secondary Education talked to me and
showed the desire to create their own play. They were already familiar
with the experience of the bilingual theatre. The first thing we did

was to have a brainstorming session in which the students proposed different topics that they were interested in. The most popular were the following: the financial crisis, unemployment, and studying and working abroad. These lead to the creation of the play, "Albojenses in the World". The play is the story of two families from Albox who emigrated to England and the United States of America. The students proposed different scenes and settings for the play and chose the parts (there were 16 characters). Then, they worked in groups writing the dialogues and structuring the scenes. At the end, the play had two stories within the same plotline: the Martinez family (the father, the pregnant mother and their daughter; she was the only one who could speak English). They go to England because the father has found a job there and the cousins (three female cousins and their friend, Antonio, who does not speak English at all) go to the USA to study at the university and work in the natural stone industry. Each of these stories had three short scenes. Because of the switches in the plot from one family to the other, there was a narrator who presented the scenes and the characters. Since the play had six scenes, the sets were complicated. Finally, we opted for a bare stage and created a video support for each scene. Eight students were in charge of research and selection of pictures from the Internet and they worked on a PowerPoint presentation to be projected during the performance of the play.

The educational contents of this play presented a rich material to be explored in the classroom. We had British and American English, so the students learnt the main differences between these two varieties of English. There were many tasks to work with the vocabulary and pronunciation. We did many exercises working with different registers of spoken English (formal-informal). One of the scenes was set in an American airport, so students learnt some vocabulary used in airports. Another scene was at the doctor's so we used it to prepare exercises to revise vocabulary on "health problems" and other questions. We encouraged the pupils to create their curricula and formal letters of application for a job in Spanish and English In some biology sessions, students could reinforce their knowledge of health problems and parts of the body. At the same time, they were provided with the new vocabulary on meat and dairy products and learn about the ones that are not allowed to be brought into the USA. Some of the sessions of the subject of social science were devoted to the study of education systems and political organizations of the United States and England. In the subject of computer science the pupils learnt how to combine visual and sound materials to give PowerPoint presentations. As to the timing, it took more than four months to write, rehearse and stage the play. The methodology of the performance is similar to the one described before. The results were positive and encouraging.

It will be unfair not to mention the difficulties we faced during the implementation of the project. On the one hand, both in the adapted and written plays there were some grammar structures that students found difficult. Some sessions were devoted to the practice of these structures. These activities were used as an extension material within the syllabus of the English subject. Another problem was the English pronunciation, and, especially, the difference between American and British oral English. Some of the pupils had problems to understand other foreign classmates speaking English. This difficulty was overcome by working on the pronunciation in small groups with the help of language assistants. The most obvious obstacle was concerned with the time the teacher had to spend on correcting and writing the play, preparing activities to work on the plays' content and to modify the syllabus. Needless to say, that this kind of project requires an extra-effort from the teacher's part. In spite of this, the result shows that it is very rewarding especially for the empathy created between the teacher and the students.

It is also important to mention the assessment process. We chose formative assessment because we were interested in the process and not in the final product. In order to evaluate the students, we used daily observation, taking into account their participation, interest and cooperation. We also considered how the students adopted their classmates' ideas in order to modify their parts and how they showed respect towards them. We checked also if the pupils used the grammar structures from the play to improve their output in oral and written English. Apart from this, the theatre activity was assessed as being part of the term activities. We assessed the pupils then, in accordance with their achievement of the basic competences. As it was mentioned before, we also had a feedback from the students and their families through the questionnaires. The teachers of other subjects gave their opinions on the theatre project and their further suggestions were collected in the report of the integrated syllabus, within the school's CLIL project. We are still working on bilingual theatre project. The results we get at the end of this school-year will be used to improve future projects.

## Conclusions

The successful performance of the bilingual plays in the foreign language class shown in this article highlights the real need for a different approach in foreign language teaching. We have achieved the specific objectives of the CLIL methodology for foreign language teaching-learning, thanks to the implementation of the theatre techniques proposed here. Combination or integration is a key concept that links theatre and CLIL, since both combine and integrate oral and written language in a natural way. We have seen that with theatre we can find many of the skills involved in the communicative act: grammatical, socio-linguistic, discursive and strategic. The performance of the plays has shown that it is very effective for improving the four communicative skills. We have experienced that the bilingual plays encourage participation and communication among pupils from different nationalities and enhance their cooperation and tolerance. This type of theatre helps pupils to overcome learning difficulties. The level of participation is very high and, as we have seen, pupils enjoy both adapting and creating their own plays. The performance is good for the actors and for the audience.

The combination of theatre and CLIL has a great potential for the explicit and implicit learning of a foreign language and its vocabulary, in addition to learning the content of a subject. The performance of these plays in the foreign language classroom provides also an interdisciplinary approach in such areas as drawing, computer science, Spanish language, social sciences, and biology. This approach takes us back to the main objectives of the CLIL methodology.

# References

Allen, J. 1979. *Drama in Schools: Its Theory and Practice*. London: Heinemann.

Baetens Beardsmore, H. 2008. Multilingualism, Cognition and Creativity. *International CLIL Research Journal* 1/1. <http://www.icrj.eu/11/article1.html> Accessed 13 April 2014.

Boudreault, C. 2010. The benefits of using drama in the ESL/EFL classroom. *The Internet TESL Journal*. <http://iteslj.org/Articles/Boudreault-Drama.html> Accessed 9 March 2014.

Bret Blasco, A. 2012. Implementing CLIL in a Primary School in Spain: The Effects of CLIL on L2 English Learners' Oral Production Skills. <http://www.recercat.net/bitstream/handle/2072/169743/Treball%20de%20recerca.pdf?sequence=1> Accessed 10 March 2014.

Burke, A. F. / O'Sullivan, J. C. 2002. *Stage by Stage: A Handbook for Using Drama in the Second Language Classroom*. Portsmouth: Heinemann.

Casal, S. / Moore, P. 2009. The Andalusian Bilingual Sections Scheme: Evaluation and Consultancy. *International CLIL Research Journal* 1/2. <http://www.icrj.eu/12/article4.html > Accessed 13 March 2014.

Corral Fullá, A. 2013. El teatro en la enseñanza de lenguas extranjeras. La dramatización como modelo y acción. *Didáctica. Lengua y Literatura* 25, 117–134.

Drew, I. 2013. Linking theatre to CLIL in foreign language education. *Nordic Journal of Modern Language Methodology* 2/1. <http://journal.uia.no/index.php/NJMLM/article/view/69#.U5r8y3a2fXQ> Accessed 10 March 2014.

Frigols Martín, M. J. 2012. CLIL implementation in Spain: an approach to different models. <http://arca.unive.it/bitstream/10278/1013/1/13Frigols.pdf> Accessed 10 April 2014.

Hardison, D. M. / Sonchaeng, C. 2005. Theatre voice training and technology in teaching oral skills: Integrating the components of a speech event. *System* 33, 593–608.

Hayers, S. K. 1984. *Drama as a Second Language: A practical guide for language teachers.* Cambridge: Cambridge University Press.

Hillyard, S. 2010. Drama and CLIL: The Power of Connection", *Humanity Language Teaching,* 12. <www.hltmag.co.uk/dec10/sart10.rtf> Accessed 12 April 2014.

Juan Rubio, A. D. / García Consea, I. M. 2012. Utilities of CLIL methodology in the classroom. *Revista de Formación e Innovación Educativa Universitaria* 5/4, 209–215.

Kao, Shin-Mei / O'Neill, C. 1998. *Words Into Worlds, Learning a Second Language through Process Drama.* Stamford: Ablex Publishing.

Lasagabaster, D. / Ruiz de Zarobe, Y. 2010. *CLIL in Spain: Implementation, Results and Teacher Training.* Cambridge Scholars Publishing, 2010.

Maley, A. / Duff, A. 2005. *Drama Techniques: A Resource Book of Communication Activities for Language Teachers.* Cambridge: Cambridge University Press.

Muszynska, A. 2012. Drama Method and Corpus Linguistics in CLIL: the Power of connection. An example of practical application in action research project *Lord of the Flies* for Secondary School level. In Breeze, R. et al. (eds). *Teaching Approaches to CLIL.* Servicio de Publicaciones de Universidad de Navarra, 235–248.

Nicolás Román, S. 2011. El teatro como recurso didáctico en la metodología CLIL: un enfoque competencial. *Encuentro* 20, 102–108.

Robinson, K. (ed). 1980. *Exploring Theatre and Education.* London: Heinemann.

Sam, W. Y. 1990. Drama in Teaching English as a Second Language- a Communicative Approach. *The English Teacher 9,* 14–21.

Smith, S. 1984. *The Theatre Arts and the Teaching of Second Languages.* London: Addison-Wesley.

Soriano Ayala, E. 2004. *La práctica educativa intercultural.* Madrid: La Muralla.

Torres Núñez, J. J. 1997. Adquisición y aprendizaje de lenguas segundas y sus literaturas. In Oro Cabanas/ I. Varela (eds). *Actas del I*

*Congreso Internacional sobre la Adquisición e aprendizaxe das linguas segundas e as súas literaturas.* Universidad de Santiago de Compostela.

_____. 1996. *Nuevos horizontes para el teatro en la enseñanza de idiomas.* Almería: Universidad de Almería.

Wessels, C. 1987. *Drama.* Oxford: Oxford University Press.

RAQUEL FERNÁNDEZ

# Readers' Theatre in the CLIL classroom

## Introduction

When Professor Amos Paran asserted that "literature" did not have a defined role in the post-communicative EFL classroom, the situation of literary texts in the classroom was more than unclear (2000: 75). However, with the advent of bilingual education, and the emergence of CLIL as a pedagogical approach, literature is faced with the opportunity of making a fresh and renewed comeback to the classroom. In Hillyard's words: "Not only do both approaches [Drama and CLIL] motivate students through engagement and connection, but also both approaches are connected in their holistic nature, engaging the whole learner experience" (2010: 1).

One of the best ways to help our students to learn any content is to get them involved in experiential learning which is meaningful for them, and helps them to contextualize the content and language they are acquiring. If there is a genre that can get students active and participative while exploring learning individually and/or collaboratively, it is drama. From the myriad of techniques available, such as role-plays, improvisations, tableaux or freeze frames, narrative pantomimes, etc., Readers' Theatre stands out for its associated benefits as demonstrated in research, which go beyond linguistic goals, and also for its simplicity, as it does not require complex or expensive materials to be implemented. Also, Readers' Theatre gives students the possibility to work on oral interpretation, scriptwriting and/or staging.

This chapter aims to present Readers' Theatre as a useful tool in the CLIL classroom to pursue not only language aims, but also educational goals. To this end, Readers' Theatre will be introduced by comparing and contrasting the available definitions. The second section of the chapter will be devoted to discussing its benefits and potential pitfalls by exploring experiences which have been carried out using Readers' Theatre around the world. In the third section, the author will justify the use of Readers' Theatre in CLIL classrooms, taking its potential advantages as the starting point and supporting its use further by connecting it with the 4 Cs stated by Do Coyle (1999). Therefore, Readers' Theatre will be considered under the light of Content, Cognition, Communication and Culture. To end with, a set of didactic guidelines regarding the use of Readers' Theatre in the CLIL classroom will be given, and steps for further research will be described to aid both those researchers interested in studying the use of Readers' Theatre and those practitioners willing to implement it in their classrooms.

## Defining Readers' Theatre

To begin with, there is no consensus about how to write its name, and many authors (see Shepard's website) consider it useful to use the initials (RT) to avoid misunderstandings. For the purposes of this paper, Readers' Theatre will be preferred rather than other options such as Reader's Theatre or Readers Theatre, as it implies that readers have a sense of belonging in the process and production of a drama activity which also requires them to work in group.

Readers' Theatre is based on the oral interpretation of a script. Students do not need to memorise the lines, as they can have the script in front of them, but their reading should be dramatic and meaningful, as the interpretation of the script given relies on the students' voices. The teacher acts as a facilitator of the discovery of the text by the reader, and the reader gives 'life' to the text. Students do not need any special scenery, costumes or props to perform their lines. However, they need to have time to "work together to produce a meaningful and entertaining performance for an audience" (Dixon 2010: 3).

Even if oral interpretation is a key component of Readers' Theatre, students may be encouraged to get involved in the creation of their own scripts. Scriptwriting can thus be incorporated as an optional element in the use of Readers' Theatre. These types of writing activities are especially useful once students know the nuts and bolts of Readers' Theatre as interpreters, as they will easily come to grips with the necessary knowledge and skills to put a script into practice. Also, it will require them to develop their negotiating skills by working in groups.

One of the main characteristics of Readers' Theatre is the absence of elements which otherwise would be common to any theatre play, such as costumes, scenery, props, etc. Even if students are not required to go on stage, it is possible to prepare Readers' Theatre staging using imagination and creativity, rather than relying on expensive materials. For instance, students can use colours to identify different characters, or change the position of their chairs to illustrate the type of relationship between the characters. They may also use digital tools to improve the creation of a dramatic atmosphere in the classroom. Even if Readers' Theatre has commonly been associated with literature and literacy development, efforts have been made to demonstrate its effectiveness when used in content subjects in monolingual settings, as demonstrated by Flynn (2004) and Mackay (2008). This trend originated the term: Content-based Readers' Theatre to refer to scripts dealing with topics included in school official curricula.

To sum up, Readers' Theatre goes beyond the idea of simply reading a script aloud in class. Quite the contrary, it involves students' active participation in class, and it demands them not only to understand the text, but also to have a sense of ownership when interpreting their lines. To do that, students need to experience what Rosenblatt (1938) defined as Transactional Reading, as they are involved in a reciprocal and mutually defining relationship. Transaction is not only individual and private, but also public and shared, as students are working in their groups to create their performances. Therefore, using Readers' Theatre in the classroom gives teachers and students the opportunity to go beyond mere decoding to explore areas such as "[…] interpreting, discussing, writing, assessing, and performing their own creative responses" (Kennedy 2011: 71).

## Benefits of using Readers' Theatre

This section is devoted to discussing the benefits and potential pitfalls of Readers' Theatre by exploring experiences which have been carried out using this method around the world. Readers' Theatre is not a new area of research, as it has been widely used in the English-speaking world for many years now. Accordingly, there exists abundant literature dealing with studies carried out to prove the benefits of using Readers' Theatre. However, most of these studies have been performed in monolingual contexts where students were not confronted with an additional language in the classroom where Readers' Theatre was used, or otherwise, they focus on ESL contexts. On the other hand, studies which analyse the benefits of Readers' Theatre in CLIL are scarce, although some timid advances working on the Norwegian context have appeared in the last few years (see Drew and Pedersen 2010; and Pettersen 2014), and valuable theoretical works are pointing to the same direction (see Hillyard 2010 and Nicolás 2011).

As has been explained in section 2, one of the main characteristics of Readers' Theatre is its interest in oral interpretation. In this light, research literature on Readers' Theatre indicates that the most obvious learning gain is reading fluency and comprehension (see Millin 1996; Rinehart 1999; Millin and Rinehart 1999; Carrick 2000; Kozub 2000; Tyler and Chard 2000; Rasinski 2003; Trainin and Andrzejczak 2006; and Visser 2013). In an EFL context, Martinez, Roser and Strecker (1999) worked with second-year Primary school children offering them the chance to work with Readers' Theatre every day for a period of 10 weeks. Results of the study show that students improved their oral reading fluency probably by use of "direct explanation, feedback and effective modelling" (1999: 334). These results reinforce the idea that if students are given the opportunity to rehearse their lines, use meaningful repetition, and are shown how to improve their interpretation, it seems coherent to find that they improve their oral fluency.

In the case of children with learning disabilities, Readers' Theatre also shows positive results in terms of reading comprehension and fluency. Corcoran and Davis (2005) studied the impact of Readers' Theatre on twelve 2nd and 3rd Year School Children with learning disabilities. The study demonstrated that not only did they improve their reading fluency scores, but also their reading attitudes and confidence level. In the same line, Caluris (n.d.) carried out a study with 35 3rd Year School Children, 5 of which had moderate to severe learning disabilities. Her study demonstrated that when children are presented with opportunities to observe modelling and repetition in a meaningful context, they improve their comprehension scores. Also, Tyler and Chard (2000) supported the idea that struggling readers feel more comfortable when repetition is part of the task. In the same line, Rinehart (1999) indicated that Readers' Theatre can make all children feel comfortable, regardless of their reading level. Doherty and Coggeshall (2005) tested the use of Readers' Theatre and storyboarding using two groups of students, one regular education and one special education. Their work demonstrates that Readers' Theatre encourages team-teaching inside groups, thus benefitting students with different profiles and learning gains. As will be argued later in this chapter, Readers' Theatre may be used as a scaffolding technique for students of all levels to enhance their reading comprehension.

Therefore, it appears that fluency gains are the first clear advantage of using Readers' Theatre in the classroom. According to Trainin and Andrzejczak (2006), there are three possible benefits we can identify as part of teaching language fluency. First, motivation, as texts are motivating and support repeated practice. Second, the "creation of a meaningful context" (2006: 2), which helps students to complete a task which may serve as a challenge for them. Also, they will strive for the best when working on prosody, including "intonation, phrasing, and attention to punctuation as the text comes to life" (2006: 2). Finally, group work, which helps students grasp meaning of the text by discussing it together.

Also in the linguistic and communicative area, Readers' Theatre has offered a number of advantages for students' writing and listening skills. Students can be involved in the rewriting of published scripts or in original scriptwriting, thus exploring their writing abilities both individually and in groups, (see Stewart, 1997; Liu, 2000; Forsythe, 1995; and Latrobe, 1996). Concerning listening, Prescott and Lewis (2003) conclude that this skill could be enhanced by using Readers' Theatre.

Readers' Theatre has also shown clear advantages regarding the learning of literature. Literary learning gains have been presented by Kennedy, who claims that Readers' Theatre helps "to bring a literary text and student closer together than what is possible with silent reading alone" (2011: 76). Kabilan and Kamaruddin (2010) designed an experiment to be carried out with 14-year-old students in Malaysia. Their aim was to determine whether students perceived that they had improved in areas such as comprehension, interest, and motivation in learning literature as a result of introducing Readers' Theatre into the class. The study revealed that students benefitted from Readers' Theatre in their understanding and motivation to learn literature.

The use of Readers' Theatre has also been proven to make a positive impact on students' attitude towards reading and on reading habits and motivation. Casey and Chamberlain (2006) demonstrated that Readers' Theatre not only improves reading fluency and oral expression, but also motivation. Worthy and Prater (2002) recorded intermediate students' conversations while preparing for Readers' Theatre. They discovered that the students were engaged in analysing the text and discussing key elements, and sometimes literary components when preparing their performance. The students' engagement was benefitted by the use of Readers' Theatre. Also Uthman (2002) indicated that students carried out one of the activities that causes them most concern and potentially fear, that is, reading aloud in a calm and collected way.

Social and cultural benefits have been highlighted by Kennedy (2011), and a core component in Zambo's (2011) didactic proposal, which highlights the role of Readers' Theatre in working on stereotypes and cliques regarding girls' self-image. Her main purpose was to improve the classroom atmosphere and the relationship students had with their peers. Readers' Theatre is in this case a tool to develop tolerance through empathy. For this purpose, the author insists on the importance of choosing the correct texts. Improvement in students' self-esteem has also been reported by Drew and Pedersen (2010), in a study with secondary school students learning English as an additional language, which proved cognitive and affective benefits for them. Also, Pettersen (2013) reported on self-esteem gains in a case study on the use of

Readers' Theatre in content based subjects in 8th Year Secondary School in Norway.

According to Dixon (2010: 5), Readers' Theatre also offers clear advantages for teachers. Teachers are helped to enhance active learning in their classroom without having to worry about money, as Readers' Theatre doesn't require the use of any expensive materials. Also, it demands teachers to leave the role of instructor and adopt the role of facilitator, which is challenging but more interesting. Readers' Theatre can incorporate the use of good-quality reading material of any genre. Besides that, teachers can help students to develop their problem-solving and social skills, by encouraging them to make group decisions. It also helps teachers to see their students' progress in a very short time.

## Readers Theatre and CLIL

One of the main concerns of this chapter is to demonstrate that Readers' Theatre can become an effective catalyser of learning in a CLIL class-room. To support this view, it is necessary to define what CLIL is and what its main components are. CLIL has been defined as a "dual-focused educational approach in which an additional language is used for the learning and teaching of both content and language" (Coyle, Hood, and Marsh 2010: 1). CLIL is divided into 4 main components which act as a sort of conceptual framework, these areas are Content, Cognition, Communication and Culture (Coyle, 1999).

### *Content*

CLIL works with a curriculum where language is integrated. Content learning is a top priority, and language should not be a barrier for students to acquire the necessary knowledge, skills and attitudes, and also it should not prevent students from being involved in the process of creating new knowledge. Content should be meaningful for students, who need to be provided with enough opportunities to develop cross-curricular contents. Thus, collaboration between content teachers and English language specialists is key to the successful implementation of CLIL. This also has an impact on students' literacy development, which should be taken into consideration in all CLIL subjects.

In the case of Readers' Theatre, scripts used can deal with any topic included in students' curriculum and/or any topic of their interest. One of the main advantages of using Readers' Theatre is that if there is not any material available, the teacher or students can create their own through creative scriptwriting.

## *Communication*

Rather than studying language in the traditional sense, students develop their linguistic skills by actually using it. A context-embedded approach is adopted, in which the students use the additional language in a variety of contexts and situations. Communication involves the development of the 4 communication skills: speaking, reading, listening and writing, through real interaction and practice. Students will cater for the three areas of the language triptych, as developed by Coyle Hood and Marsh (2010: 9–10), which includes: language of learning, for learning and through learning.

Readers' Theatre involves language in different levels. First, students need to express their opinions and negotiate meaning in the process of planning their reading performance and/or when involved in scriptwriting. Second, they are required to understand the text that they will represent in different levels. On the one hand, students need to become acquainted with different reading, which is focused on the literal meaning of words. On the other hand, they will pay attention to those nuances which make their reading a unique transaction with the text, as they are also dealing with representational language (see Rosenblatt, "Continuing the Conversation: A Clarification" for a discussion about this continuum). Third, when involved in scriptwriting, the students are allowed to explore the associations of speech and characters. For example, they need to come to terms with what type of vocabulary, specific prosodic features or set phrases a given character will have. In some cases, this will lead them to go back to the text given as a primary source. For instance, if they are developing a script from a literary text, they will probably pay attention to recurrent expressions used by the characters. In other cases, they will need to come up with ideas from scratch, above all when they are creating new characters. Finally, there will be some cases in which they need to pay attention to metaphorical meanings, for example, the way in which a cloud will talk.

## Cognition

Cognitive development is a key issue in CLIL. As students will not have their contents watered down just because they are taught using an additional language, cognitive work needs to be addressed appropriately. Students will be faced with managing cognitively challenging work just as they do in their mother tongue. To do this, teachers should use scaffolding appropriately. Scaffolding is understood as "a process of 'setting up' the situation to make the child's entry easy and successful and then gradually pulling back and handing the role to the child as he becomes skilled enough to manage it" (Bruner 1983: 60). Also, it is important to foster students' divergent thinking, and their work on High-Order Thinking Skills, as proposed by Bloom and revised by Anderson and Krathwohl. In this sense, it is also important to help students to reflect on their own practice to be able to recognise achievements and suggest improvements.

Readers' Theatre also responds to the different learning styles of children. In light of Gardner's Multiple Intelligences Theory (1999), Readers' Theatre has the potential to develop every type of intelligence:

- Musical-rhythmic: students can explore prosodic features: intonation, pronunciation, pitch, which may influence how we convey meaning and also our construction of characters.
- Visual-spatial: students have a strong visual memory, and it is easy for them to imagine the scenes which are part of the dialogue while writing the script or during the performance. They also incorporate spatial elements into the performance.
- Verbal-linguistic: students with this preferred learning style feel at ease working with words. They will pay attention to

vocabulary and grammar use, and will be actively involved in the scriptwriting activities.

– Logical-mathematical: due to their high abstract and critical thinking, they tend to value their peers' points of view and try to reach an agreement. They are also good at making sequences and developing plots.

– Bodily-kinaesthetic: even if scripts are not thought to be represented on stage, bodily-kinaesthetic students will add movements and gestures, sometimes even inadvertently, to enhance understanding.

– Interpersonal: most Readers' Theatre techniques are based on cooperative learning and group work. Students will need to cope with a variety of situations, from negotiating meaning from the text to reaching agreements on the roles to play.

– Intrapersonal: students who prefer this type of intelligence tend to use introspective techniques and are self-reflective. This will help them foresee the emotions and feelings of the characters that they are going to play. Also, they will consider which of their own personal skills could be useful both in the group work and in the performance.

– Naturalistic: natural explorers will feel at ease adding contextualising elements to the performance and further investigating characteristics of the roles they have to perform. They will also be aware of a more global understanding of their piece of work.

One obvious cognitive advantage of using Readers' Theatre is that it can be used as a support for the six main types of instructional scaffolding as identified by Walqui (2006: 170–177): modelling, bridging, contextualisation, building schema, re-representing text and developing metacognition. If Readers' Theatre is to be applied effectively, students involved in the task must be offered with plenty of modelling, usually facilitated by guided rehearsals and meaningful repetition. Also, students need to connect their previous knowledge with new knowledge, often by transferring the information they know to a different format. This involves bridging, building schema and re-representing text. Thus, students reading a text about 'The Water Cycle' may write a script in which all the implied elements are engaged in a dialogue which describes this process. Students need to have prior knowledge of the subject, agree on what they know, share it with the rest, and convert this knowledge into words which will form the lines of each character. Also, they will be involved in the process of analysing and evaluating their performances to improve the script and the performance, thus developing their meta-cognitive skills. Finally, Readers' Theatre facilitates the best conditions to promote long-term learning by giving students the possibility to contextualise what they know and getting them active in the creation of their own knowledge.

*Culture*

Culture is sometimes identified as Community and/or Citizenship. It is an area which requires students to develop tolerance, understanding and empathy with other cultures and points of view. It promotes multicultural awareness and understanding by reinforcing "global citizenship". Culture takes a step beyond reading about English traditions to explore beliefs, customs and concerns in a pluricultural society.

Drama is an invaluable tool to encourage students to put themselves in others' shoes. Students are required to adopt a role and perspective which can be very different from the one they have in real life. They are faced with different contexts and settings in the past, present and future. Students will then be faced with situations which require them to think critically and manage all the variables involved. By giving students the opportunity to get to know other points of view, we are enriching their cultural awareness and promoting understanding.

One important issue which is important to cover when dealing with CLIL is literacy development. This key area should form a core part of the curriculum of English language subjects developed in CLIL programmes. The language teacher should also be involved in an English language curriculum with matches the needs and progress of the students in the content subjects (see Halbach 2014: 1–14).

# Implementing Readers' Theatre in the CLIL Classroom

In this section a set of didactic guidelines regarding the use of Readers' Theatre in the CLIL classroom will be given. Readers Theatre can be implemented in the classroom in a variety of ways, from which I have distinguished three main implementation models: traditional model, CLIL teacher-guided model, CLIL student-centred model.

## *Traditional model*

The traditional model is what many teachers already do intuitively in their classes. They start the lesson by saying that a performance will be prepared in the lesson. They have photocopies of the script which are handed out. The students read the script in silence, and the teacher nominates roles. The teacher gives some time for students to rehearse and the performance is carried out. In some cases, the topic of the Readers' Theatre script can be related to the curriculum but emphasis on this point is not made.

## *CLIL teacher-guided model*

For a Readers' Theatre to be CLIL one essential point is that the contents included in the script should be related to a topic in the curriculum or a cross-curricular element. The teacher starts the lesson with an activation of prior knowledge activity, depending on the topic they are dealing with. Then, the students are asked to imagine what would happen if X and Y (aspects, elements, animals, people, etc.) met in a specific place, thus defining the context of the Readers' Theatre script. Then, the students are told that the teacher has the lines for each character, and a list of characters participating in the dialogue is read out. The students decide which role they would like to be, giving their justifications accordingly. The teacher gives the script to the students, leaving dictionaries, laptops and other language aids at hand to solve their questions regarding vocabulary and pronunciation. The teacher can limit the number of words she can help with to ten, for example.

Later, the students are given time to rehearse their lines individually. They can change places, work with a partner if they feel it is more comfortable, or they can use other places in the school (if possible). Once this is done, the students undertake their first group rehearsal. It is very important for the teacher not to intervene in this first rehearsal (unless it is a complete disaster), as the students will negotiate how to create the performance. They will ask each other about the meaning of words, their pronunciation, and will discuss how to say them properly. They will give suggestions to each other to improve the performance. The students are then given time for a second rehearsal in which the teacher should monitor that everybody is participating. Then, time for a third group rehearsal can be given, suggesting students to go to another place or use a corner in the room. When they are ready, they perform the dialogue sitting down, in a circle. This is very important because they can see each other's faces. They comment on the performance and how it can be improved. Some time is given for them to practise alone and polish up these aspects. A second chance to represent their script is given. This time it can be recorded, if they agree.

Once this has been considered, the main differences between the first model and the second are that:

- Students are working on a script related to a topic in the curriculum.
- Students are experiencing this drama activity as part of the planning for a content topic.
- Students are given time to explore the text individually or in pairs.
- Students are given time to negotiate meaning and give feedback.
- Students are given opportunities to rehearse and improve their first version.

## CLIL student-centred model

This is an enhanced model of implementation of Readers' Theatre. In this case, it is advisable to previously train students in the use of Readers' Theatre with models 1 and 2. If students feel at ease practising Readers' Theatre script, it will be much easier to carry out this activity in the classroom.

There are many ways in which students can receive the input they will need to create their scripts. You can extract a text from a textbook, you can show them a picture, you can give them just the first line of the script, you can give them the setting, you can create the setting physically in class, you can play a sound or sounds in class. Input can be multimodal, it can be new or already known by the students. The most important thing is that it encourages students to activate their prior knowledge, and that the focus quickly on the task.

Once the input or prompt is given, the students are asked to brainstorm about the characters which may appear in the dialogue. If the students already have the characters, they can talk about the setting and the main plot. Once this is done, they will have time to think about which character they would like to perform and justify why. The students will decide who will play which character, and will then start creating their dialogues. To do this, the teacher will remind them about the plot, the setting and the characters, and will leave textbooks, laptops, and dictionaries at hand.

Students will devote one or two sessions to the writing of the script. Once this is done, the script will be given to the teacher or to another group in order to produce feedback. Students will take their recommendations into account and start working on their roles. The number of group rehearsals needed will vary according to the students' experience in using Readers' Theatre. Normally, they will require three rehearsals to be ready for their first performance. An audio recording can be made so that students can listen to and improve upon the performance. If the students are experienced, or if there are many bodily-kinaesthetic students in the group, they will suggest adding gestures. You can give the students the possibility of standing up and making gestures to back up meaning. Not all of them will feel comfortable with this idea, therefore, let them explore this possibility and reject it if they do not want to do it. It is very important that they find their way in acting out Readers' Theatre. The last Readers' Theatre representation can be videotaped and used as input material for this or other groups.

During the process of creating a Readers' Theatre script, teachers and students can be aided by ICT, thus integrating its use in a natural way. This can be done from the early stages in the preparation, for example, the teacher can use padlet.com to organise students' ideas digitally. Students can have access to their classmates' ideas instantly by using laptops, tablets, mobile phones or the IWB.

Times have also changed for video and audio recording in class. Years ago, teachers had to buy expensive cameras and tape recorders, and after all the effort, the quality was not very good. Today we can record using mobile phones. Students can show their friends and parents what they have been doing in class that same morning. In the case of audio recording, the audio files can be edited and stored using Audacity. Also, students can use the audio recordings to generate comics or representations by using websites such as Animoto.

Audio can also be a good addition to a Readers' Theatre performance. Students can download sound effects and add them while they are performing their role play. This will increase the importance of audio input while representing. Some students prefer to use some background music to get their audience inspired. For example, a group of primary students decided to use a The Lord of The Rings' piece to represent the Water Cycle, as the music gave them the feeling of adventure.

Regarding visuals, it is true that Readers' Theatre is famous for not needing any special props. I have seen how a group of students have created props for a Readers' Theatre in order to get into role simply by using head scarfs and elements found in class. It is also possible to use the Interactive Whiteboard to recreate the setting of the story. Children enjoy this activity immensely, and it gives the teacher the chance to brush up on their knowledge of both content and language.

Tablets can also be a great way to support students' scripts. They can use them instead of paper if they feel more comfortable. It can also be used as a way to jot down any symbols or lines that they come up with. Digital tools can also be used to create Powerpoint presentations where the script has been previously recorded, to which, the visuals are then added. Another alternative is to use programmes which help you to create stories very easily, such as PuppetPals or ZooBurst, which enables you to create a four-dimensional book.

## Useful resources to get started with Reader's Theatre

This section intends to provide a brief bibliographical guide of useful resources which can help teachers and researchers to implement Reader's Theatre in their classrooms. In order to facilitate their access, only digitally available resources have been compiled.

- *Aaron Shepard's Readers' Theatre Page* is one of the most comprehensive sites devoted to the use of Readers' Theatre. It contains an introduction to the use of Reader's Theatre, tips, examples of performances carried out with scripts, scripts that you can download and use in your classes, and useful downloadable materials to start scriptwriting in your lessons. Also, Shepard has compiled a useful bibliography for teachers and researchers to further explore the use of Reader's Theatre in their classes. The website can be visited here: http://www.aaronshep.com/rt/index. html
- *Fiction Teachers* claims to be the Number One Site for Fiction Teachers on the Web. It includes sections on poetry, fiction and theatre (classroom theatre). Here you can find tips and recommendations on how to use theatre in your lessons, and lesson plans and scripts available to be used in class. They are classified according to the educational levels they are directed at. The website is: http://www.fictionteachers.com/classroomtheater/ theater.html
- *Stories to Grow By* is a fantastic site for teachers interested in working with stories in their classrooms. It contains a specific section on Readers' Theatre where you can access a variety of scripts, most of them adapted from traditional folktales and fairytales from around the world. Each script indicates the number of people needed to perform the story. The website can be visited here: http://www.storiestogrowby.com/script.html

- *Reader's Theater Scripts and Plays* is a website which supports the use of Reader's Theatre as a valid tool to help children gain reading fluency. They encourage the use of scripts in classrooms, and have created them for use at Key Stage 3 level. You can access their compilation of scripts here: http://teachingheart.net/readerstheater.htm
- *PBS Kids* stands for children's programming produced by the Public Broadcasting Service in the United States. Their website includes a section with a collection of scripts which can be used in schools. You can find it here: http://pbskids.org/zoom/activities/playhouse/
- *Scripts for Schools* is a site created by author Lois Walker. Despite not all the scripts being free, as a starting point, it is worth browsing this fantastic compilation and downloading the available titles. The scripts are organised into different categories according to topics or genre, for example: "Fables, myths and legends" and "Asian Tales". The site can be accessed here: http://www.scriptsforschools.com
- *Story Cart* is described as 'Your Source for Readers Theatre and More', and it has been designed for use at elementary school levels. There are free scripts available for visitors to download and use. Website: http://www.storycart.com
- *The Best Class* was launched as a website to improve communication between parents, students and teachers. It now offers the possibility to access scripts created to be used in class. You can visit it here: http://www.thebestclass.org/rtscripts.html

This is just a small selection of resources which can be accessed quickly using the Internet. However, teachers and students do not need external resources to implement Readers' Theatre in class, as they can create their own scripts and then make them available to other students and teachers.

## Conclusions

In this paper, the role of Readers' Theatre in the CLIL classroom has been supported by considering its main features. The aim has been to examine the main aspects of CLIL, and reflect upon how we can make them work together harmoniously in order to make bilingual education reach the highest goals. According to literature in the field, the use of drama can bring about significant learning gains in students, which go beyond language and communication skills, to cater for cognitive, cultural and content-specific learning goals. If drama is to bring so much joy into the CLIL classroom, its purported lack of use may be caused by teachers' lack of knowledge and/or training. Therefore, it would be interesting to develop specialised training courses and materials to help teachers to see the educational value of using Readers' Theatre as a drama technique in their CLIL classrooms.

Furthermore, it is also important to highlight that the first steps of empirical research regarding the use of Readers' Theatre in CLIL Classrooms have already been taken (see Drew and Pedersen 2010; and Pettersen 2013). Hopefully, in the near future, the preliminary results will allow us to redefine and improve the use of Reader's Theatre in the bilingual context. Therefore, it is important to help teachers to think about its use and make results available to the research community.

One important research area to be explored is the use of Readers' Theatre with students with learning needs. Within this scope, we can find a variety of student needs and profiles. It would be very helpful to distinguish between different learning needs and check whether Readers' Theatre is helping students reach their learning goals, considering certain characteristics. Students with dyslexia are indeed very different from students diagnosed with Hyperactivity or Autism Spectrum Disorders. Each student may benefit in a different way from the use of Readers' Theatre and, in some cases, its use may be advised against.

Concerning the use of Readers' Theatre, many empirical studies have obtained positive results regarding motivation levels in students' performance in class. However, this increase in motivation may be caused by the introduction of an innovative element into the class, which creates a sense of distance from traditional classes. Therefore, it would be interesting to know if this motivation is maintained through time when Reader's Theatre becomes mainstream practice in the classroom.

In the realm of CLIL contexts, it would be interesting to discover whether Readers' Theatre contributes to learning development in all content-areas, and whether it can be used as a 'bridge' between the English language subject and the content subjects. Also, it would be interesting to find out if the students' language development increases with higher exposure to Readers' Theatre. More specifically, student writing skills could be the main focus of a longitudinal research to explore how children increase their linguistic and communicative abilities through writing with the use of Readers' Theatre. The research could also study to what extent the students' improved writing skills have an impact on their acquisition of content and creation of meaning.

Together, CLIL and Drama present students with the challenge of actively participating in class, not only acquiring knowledge, but also creating meaning and contributing to the lesson by offering up their experiences and beliefs. They both encourage cognitive development through the use of critical thinking and multiple intelligences, and are also sensitive to cultural and moral issues which will be essential to educate children as citizens. If Drama can boost CLIL's educational goals, it is time to consider how drama techniques can be implemented in the classroom to create a perfect synergy.

# References

Anderson, L. W. / Krathwohl, D.R. 2001. *A Taxonomy for Learning, Teaching and Assessing: A Revision of Bloom's Taxonomy of Educational Objectives.* New York: Addison Wesley Longman.

Bloom, B. S. 1984. *Taxonomy of Educational Objectives.* New York: Longman.

Bruner, J. 1983. *Child's Talk.* New York: Norton.

Caluris, J. Using Readers Theater to Show Off Good Reading. *Teachers Network*, ActionResearch. (n.d.). <http://teachersnetwork.org/ tnli/research/achieve/caluris.pdf > Accessed 3 May 2014.

Carrick, L. U. 2000. *The effects of Readers Theatre on fluency and comprehension in fifth grade students in regular classrooms.* Dissertation. Lehigh University.

Casey, S. / Chamberlain, R. 2006. Bringing reading alive through readers theatre. *Illinois Reading Council Journal* 34, 17–25.

Corcoran, C. / Davis, A. 2005. A Study on the Effects of Readers' Theatre on Second and Third Grade Special Education Students' Fluency Growth. *Reading Improvement* 42/2, 103–111.

Coyle, D. / Hood, P. / Marsh, D. 2010. *Content and Language Integrated Learning.* Cambridge: Cambridge University Press.

Coyle, D. 1999. Supporting students in content and language integrated learning contexts. planning for effective classrooms. In J. Masih (ed). *Learning Through a Foreign Language: models, methods and outcomes.* London, UK: Centre for Information on Language Teaching and Research, 46–62.

Dixon, N. 2010. *Readers Theatre: A Secondary Approach.* Winnipeg: Portage and Main Press.

Doherty, J. / Coggeshall, K. 2005. Reader's Theater and Storyboarding: Strategies that Include and Improve. *Voices from the Middle* 12/4, 37–43.

Drew, I. / Pedersen, R.R. 2010. Readers Theatre: A different approach to English for struggling readers. *Acta Didactica Norge* 4, 1–18.

Flynn, R. 2004. Curriculum-based reader's theater: Setting the stage for reading and retention. *The Reading Teacher* 58/4, 360–365.

Forsythe, S. 1995. It worked! Readers theatre in second grade (teaching reading). *The Reading Teacher* 49/3, 264–265.

Gardner, H. 1999. *Intelligence Reframed: Multiple Intelligences for the 21st Century.* New York: Basic Books.

Halbach, A. 2014. Teaching (in) the foreign language in a CLIL context: Towards a new approach. In R. Breeze et al (eds). *Integration of theory and practice in CLIL.* Amsterdam: Rodopi, 1–14.

Hillyard, S. 2010. Drama and CLIL: The Power of Connection. *Humanising Language Teaching Magazine* 12/6 <www.hltmag.co.uk/ dec10/sart10.rtf> Accessed 3 April 2014.

Kabilan, M. K. / Kamaruddin, F. 2010. Engaging learners' comprehension, interest, and motivation to learn literature using the reader's theatre. *English Teaching Practice and Critique* 9/3, 132–159. http://files.eric.ed.gov/fulltext/EJ912627.pdf> accessed 15 May 2014.

Kennedy, J. 2011. Oral Interpretation of Literature: Readers' Theater. *The CEA Forum* Winter/Spring, 71–77. < http://files.eric.ed.gov/fulltext/EJ985752.pdf> Accessed 3 April 2014.

Kozub, R. 2000. Reader's Theater and Its Effect on Oral Language Fluency. *Reading online* August <http://www.readingonline.org/editorial/edit_index.asp?HREF=august2000/rkrt.htm > Accessed 10 May 2014.

Latrobe, K. 1996. Encouraging reading and writing through readers theatre. *Emergency librarian* 23/3, 16–20.

Liu, J. 2000. The Power of Readers Theatre: from Reading to Writing. *ELT Journal* 54/4, 354–361. < http://203.72.145.166/ELT/files/54-4-6.pdf> Accessed 3 April 2014.

Mackay, M. E. 2008. Readers Theatre – Take Another Look – It's More than Fluency Instruction. *LEARNing Landscapes* 2/1, 131–144. <http://www.portageandmainpress.com/author_article/a_11.pdf> Accessed 3 April 2014.

Martínez, M. / Roser, N. L. / Strecker, S. 1999. "I Never Thought I Could Be a Star": A Readers Theatre Ticket to Fluency. *The Reading Teacher* 52/ 4, 326–334. <www.tc.pbs.org/.../docs/c1s3_11inever thought.pdf> Accessed 10 April 2014.

Millin, S. K. / Rinehart, S. D. 1999. Some of the benefits of readers theater participation for second-grade Title I students. *Reading Research and Instruction* 39/1, 71–88.

Millin, S. K. 1996. *Effect of Readers Theatre on oral reading ability and reading attitudes of second grade Title 1 students*. Unpublished Doctoral Dissertation. West Virginia University.

Nicolás Román, S. 2011. El teatro como recurso didáctico en la metodología CLIL: un enfoque competencial. *Encuentro* 20, 102–108. <http://dspace.uah.es/dspace/bitstream/handle/10017/10111/teatro_nicolas_ENCUENTRO_2011.pdf?sequence=1> Accessed 10 April 2014.

Paran, A. 2000. Survey review: Recent books on the teaching of literature. *ELT Journal* 54/1, 75–88.

Pettersen, S. R. 2013. *A Case Study of a content-based Readers Theatre Project in an 8th Grade EFL class in Norway.* MS Thesis. Hogskolen i Ostfold. <http://brage.bibsys.no/xmlui/bitstream/id/109118/Pettersen1.pdf > Accessed 10 May 2014.

Prescott, J. / Lewis, M. 2003. The power of readers theatre. *Instructor* 11, 22–29. <http://www.scholastic.com/teachers/article/power-readers-theater> Accessed 10 May 2014.

Rasinski, T. V. 2003. *The Fluent Reader: Oral Reading Strategies for Building Word Recognition, Fluency, and Comprehension.* New York: Scholastic.

Rinehart, S. 1999. Don't think for a minute that I'm getting up there: Opportunities for reader's theatre in a tutorial for children with reading problems. *Journal of Reading Psychology* 20, 71–89.

Rosenblatt, L. M. 1995. *Literature as Exploration.* New York: Appleton-Century.

Rosenblatt, L.M. 1995. Continuing the Conversation: A Clarification. *Research in the Teaching of English* 29/3, 349–354.

Shepard, A. *Aaron Shepard's Home Page.* < http://www.aaronshep.com/> Accessed 10 May 2014.

Stewart, L. 1997. Readers Theatre and the Writing Workshop: Using Children's Literature to Prompt Student Writing. *Reading Teacher* 51/2, 174–175.

Trainin, G. / Andrzejczak, N. 2006. Readers' Theatre: A Viable Reading Strategy?. *American Educational Research Association meeting.* University of Nebraska. <http://cehs.unl.edu/artslinc/researchandevalutation/files/publications/readerstheatre.pdf> Accessed 10 May 2014.

Tyler, B. / Chard, D. 2000. Using Readers Theatre to Foster Fluency in Struggling Readers: A Twist on the Repeated Reading Strategy. *Reading and Writing Quarterly* 16, 163–168.

Uthman, L. E. 2002. Readers' Theatre: An Approach to reading with more than a touch of drama. *Teaching PreK-8,* 32/6, 56–57.

Visser, T. E. 2013. *The effects of readers theatre on the reading comprehension, fluency and motivation of the elementary English language learning student.* Ms Diss. Northern Michigan University.

<http://www.nmu.edu/education/sites/DrupalEducation/files/UserFiles/Visser_Tara_MP.pdf> Accessed 20 May2014.

Walqui, A. 2006. Scaffolding Instructions for English Language Learners: A Conceptual Framework. *The International Journal of Bilingual Education and Bilingualism* 9/2, 159–180. <http://www.educacion.gob.es/exterior/centros/losangeles/es/series/201003-Scaffolding-Walqui.pdf> Accessed 20 May. 2014.

Worthy, J. / Prater, K. 2002. "I thought about it all night" Readers theatre for reading fluency and motivation. *The Reading Teacher* 56, 294–297.

Zambo, D. 2011. Young Girls Discovering their Voice with Literacy and Readers Theatre. *Young Children* 66/2, 28–35. <http://www.naeyc.org/files/yc/file/201103/ReadersTheater_Zambo_Online0311.pdf> Accessed 10 May 2014.

# List of Tables and Figures

# Notes on Contributors

CEM BALCIKANLI works as an Associate Professor in the ELT Department, Gazi Faculty of Education at Gazi University in Turkey and is the vice director of the School of Foreign Languages at the same university. He taught Turkish in the University of Florida between 2008 and 2009 as a Fulbright scholar. He completed his PhD degree at Gazi University in 2010. He has been the editor in chief of the Journal of Language Learning and Teaching (www.jltl.org) since 2011. His professional interests include learner/teacher autonomy, the role of technology in language learning/teaching, teaching Turkish as a second language, second language teacher education. He has widely published in international journals "Learner Autonomy in Language Learning: Student Teachers' Beliefs" (*Australian Journal of Teacher Education*, 2010), "Learning to foster autonomy: The role of teacher education materials"-with Reinders (*SISAL Journal*, 2011), "Metacognitive Awareness Inventory For Teachers" (*Electronic Journal of Research in Educational Psychology*, 2011), and "The Use of the EPOSTL to Foster Teacher Autonomy: ELT Student Teachers' and Teacher Trainers' Views"- with Çakır (*Australian Journal of Teacher Education*-2012) and presented in international conferences around the world.

LENI DAM is Coordinator of the LA Special Interest Group (IATEFL). In 1973, she took her first steps towards developing learner autonomy with a group of 14-year-old mixed-ability students learning English at a comprehensive school south of Copenhagen. In the following years, language learner autonomy was developed in all her classes at primary as well as secondary level. In 1979, she combined teaching at school with a job as an educational adviser and in-service teacher trainer at University College, Copenhagen till she retired in 2006. In 2004, she was awarded an honorary doctorate in pedagogy by Karlstad University, Sweden. Together with Lienhard Legenhausen, Münster University, Germany, she has studied the linguistic development of learners in autonomous classroom environments. Her areas of interest are the development of learner autonomy, differentiated teaching and learning, internal evaluation and the use of logbooks and portfolios. Within these areas, she has produced materials, written articles and books, and given numerous talks in many different countries. She is now freelance.

RAQUEL FERNÁNDEZ is a university lecturer working at Centro Universitario Cardenal Cisneros (CUCC) (Alcalá de Henares, Madrid), where she has been recently appointed Deputy Director (Educational Innovation and Research). She is also a lecturer for the Master in TEFL (University of Alcalá), in charge of a subject related to the use of short stories for creative language teaching. From 2009 to 2014, she has been in charge of an innovation project, coordinating the Bilingual Project at CUCC. She holds a Ph.D from Universidad de Alcalá since 2006, and her main fields of interest are the use of literature in the EFL/CLIL classroom, the development of literacy in bilingual contexts and CLIL provision for Infant and Primary teachers. Her Doctoral Dissertation, published by @becedario with the title "El uso de la literatura en la enseñanza del inglés como lengua extranjera", revolves around the use of literature in Secondary Education. In 2013, she was awarded with a BEDA Prize with a didactic project about the development of CLIL awareness in Higher Education. Also, she has collaborated as a pedagogical advisor for Edelvives and Vicens Vives, and has worked as content creator and speaker for University of Dayton Publishing.

NAILYA GARIPOVA holds a PhD in English Philology (University of Almeria). She is a Secondary School teacher with experience on staging plays at different educational levels. Her main research areas are: Language and culture of English speaking countries, Russian literature and culture and its influence on English fiction and Pedagogical approaches of teaching English as L2 through literature. She serves in the executive and editorial board of the international department of the literary journal *The Blue Orange* (Saint Petersburg). She is a member of the Russian Association of Writers and Nabokov French Society.

SUSAN HILLYARD is Coordinator for Teaching English through Drama in Special Education, Ministry of Education, City of Buenos Aires, Argentina where she is based. She was a NILE Associate trainer and the Executive Editor for Development of the LACLIL on-line Journal.

She has co-authored "Global Issues" an RBT for OUP. She has written materials for *Inglés, Inglês, English: ESP for South American Teachers* for the British Council and co-authored the TDI-TKT on-line course for Pearson, New York. Susan likes to teach and moderate on-line, especially for TESOL's EVO Drama courses and to deliver presentations at conferences and lead workshops on, amongst other topics, developing ELT through Drama, CLIL and Global Issues, Leadership and Management. Trained at Warwick University, UK, in the heyday of Educational Drama, growing with Dorothy Heathcote's *Drama as a Learning Medium*, she has lived in and taught EFL/ESL in five countries and has work experience in a further twelve.

DONNA LEE FIELDS has a Ph.D in Spanish literature and is a Professor at the International University of Valencia, Spain. She specializes in the CLIL method and magisterial classes. She is a teacher-trainer and gives talks on teaching methods and the philosophy and creative tools to use to stimulate virtual classes. She has published articles and papers internationally on distance learning and the CLIL method. Coordinator for the on-line English courses at the Diputación of Valencia, and examiner for level exams at the Conselleria d'Educació in Valencia. She has taught primary, secondary and adult classes in public and private schools both in the United States and in Spain and currently working on a book about the role of the witch in fairy tales from a philosophical/psychological perspective.

PATRICIA MARTÍN ORTIZ is Associate Professor of English at the University of Salamanca where she teaches English Language and Children's Literature. She received her degree in English Philology in 1994 at the University of Salamanca where she earned her PhD in 2002. Her main fields of interest are teaching English language to young learners, literature and literacy in Early English Language Education and children's literature. She has been English Teacher in Secondary School since 1996. She has published books such as *Language Teaching: Theoretical Basis and Curricular Design*, *The Golden Tree of 19th and Early 20th Century Children's Literature in English*, *English and American Literature. A Practical Approach* and *La literatura infantil en Roald Dahl*.

Tomás Motos Teruel has a Ph.D in Philosophy and the Science of Education, as well as a degree in Psychology. Professor and Lecturer of Didactics and Educational Management at University of Valencia, for more than twenty years. Now retired he is even more active, as the Director of "Theatre in Education: Theatrical Pedagogy" at the University of Valencia and a teacher on various postgraduate courses, He gives teacher-training courses, seminars and lectures in different countries, and participates in national and international congresses. He has authored books and papers and has collaborated on publications on Creativity, Body Language, Theatre in Education, Arts Education, Social Theatre, and Teaching of Language and Literature. His latest publication is "Otros escenarios para el Teatro" (2013). A playwright as well, his most recent work is "Sylvia, leona de Dios", on the life of American poet Sylvia Plath. At the moment, his main focus has been in Applied Theatre, working with the company "Teatro Playback Inestable" in Valencia.

Kemal Sinan Özmen currently works as a faculty member at Gazi University, English language teaching program in Turkey. He holds a PhD degree on teaching English as a foreign language with a specific focus on pre-service teacher education. Dr. Özmen also studied at University of Rochester, Warner School of Education as a Fulbright PhD visiting researcher. His research interests are centered on teacher cognition including variables such as teacher beliefs, teacher identity, critical thinking and teaching as a performing art. Some of his relevant publications are: 'Exploring student-teachers' beliefs about language learning and teaching' (*Current Issues in Education*, 2012), 'Washback and teacher burnout' (*The Teacher Trainer Journal*, 2012), 'The impact of and acting course on prospective teachers' beliefs about language teaching' (*Eurasian Journal of Educational Research*, 2011) and 'Fostering nonverbal immediacy and teacher identity through an acting course' (*Australian Journal of Teacher Education*, 2010).

# Linguistic Insights

## Studies in Language and Communication

· · · · · · · · · · · · · · · · ·

This series aims to promote specialist language studies in the fields of linguistic theory and applied linguistics, by publishing volumes that focus on specific aspects of language use in one or several languages and provide valuable insights into language and communication research. A cross-disciplinary approach is favoured and most European languages are accepted.

The series includes two types of books:

– **Monographs** – featuring in-depth studies on special aspects of language theory, language analysis or language teaching.
– **Collected papers** – assembling papers from workshops, conferences or symposia.

Each volume of the series is subjected to a double peer-reviewing process.

*Editorial address:*

Prof. Maurizio Gotti    Università di Bergamo, Dipartimento di Lingue, Letterature
                        Straniere e Comunicazione, Piazza Rosate 2, 24129 Bergamo, Italy
                        Fax: +39 035 2052789, E-Mail: m.gotti@unibg.it